# THE
# INTERNATIONAL
# SALES HANDBOOK

# JOHN LYNCH

This version first printed 2014

Published by Mandrill Press www.mandrillpress.com

ISBN 978-1-910194-05-8

*To Joe, with thanks for his help on financial matters*

*and*

*Pauline from Essex Freight in Sheffield, without whose expertise in shipping goods all over the world and solving the problems that arise I would have found the last fifteen years much more difficult than they have been*

# Contents

# Chapter 1:
# International Sales

For more than forty years, I have made a good living in international sales. I've lived and worked on every continent except Antarctica. In this book I'm going to tell you how I did it—do it, in fact, because I haven't retired yet. This is a practical handbook. I'm not going to tell you how it should be; I'm going to tell you how it is.

Some of what I say can, if the reader is so minded, be interpreted as racism. Don't expect an apology. The purpose of this book is not to talk about how we'd like things to be, or how the vicar or the social worker tells us they are; the object is to warn you of the traps and pitfalls that lie in wait when you do business in someone else's country, and pretending they don't exist will not be helpful.

## What is 'International Sales', anyway?

When I talk about international sales, I mean selling something—anything—outside your own country. If you're American and you sell to Europe—that's international sales. If you're British and you sell to Germany—that's international sales. It may not feel as different or as exotic as selling to Indonesia or China or Oman, but it's still international sales. What I aim to do in this book is tell you how to get the best results and (so far as you can) avoid risk.

John Lynch

## *What do you need to be an international salesperson?*

This is not a How To Sell book. There are lots of those; some are really good and some are no help at all. I won't be telling you how to recognise a buying signal or handle objections because if you can't do those things you shouldn't be attempting to sell outside your own country anyway. You'll be on your own, miles from home with no-one to help you or haul you out of any mess you land yourself in—so get the learning-how-to-sell bit done before you start getting visas in your passport. What you probably need to know is that selling in someone else's country is not so different from selling in your own. European, Asian, Canadian or Brazilian; Hindu, Moslem, Christian or atheist; people buy from people. If you've mastered the art of persuading the people you grew up among, you have what it takes to do the same with strangers. There are some things you need to know that you haven't come across in your life so far; explaining what they are and how to deal with them is what this book is about.

## *Languages*

Do you need them? Yes and no. It's always good to know what's going on around you but languages are more important in some countries than in others; also, there's the question of what your own native language is. There are probably more Chinese speakers in the world than speakers of any other language, but Chinese won't get you very far once you leave China. If you're an English speaker, though, you're one of the lucky people because English is very widely spoken. Spanish and French speakers will also do well.

### English Speakers

If you're going to be selling in the UK, Ireland, the USA, Canada (outside Quebec), South Africa, Nigeria, Ghana, Kenya, Tanzania, Uganda, Australia, New Zealand or most of the Caribbean the majority of your customers will speak English as

2

a first language. In India and Pakistan anyone in a position to do business with you will be fluent in English.

Go to the Middle East and you'll find that Arabic is the predominant language (with local variations—Farsi (Persian) in Iran; Turkish in Turkey; a language similar to Farsi in parts of Kurdistan), but English is so widely spoken as to make communication with businessmen and government people very easy for English speakers. For years, my biggest customer in Saudi Arabia has had a policy that the company's operating language is English, and that is by no means unusual there.

In parts of Asia, including China, a mastery of English is less common than many people imagine and you may need an interpreter.

Europe is mixed. In Scandinavia, Italy, Spain and Portugal, educated people probably speak English. That's also true in France, though the French may pretend not to when you're there. Quite a lot of their peers in Germany and Switzerland don't speak English. In Eastern Europe, the amount of spoken English varies but the people you want to do business with have probably mastered it because they have always known they would have to. If you want to be successful in Russia, you really need to speak Russian.

But that business about France reminds us of an advantage to being multilingual that is often overlooked. Even when people are talking to you in your language, they're probably speaking to each other in their own—and it can be amazing to discover how often what they say to each other differs from what they are telling you. I have found it very useful to look blank while listening to the Frenchmen, who were so cordial when speaking English to me, discussing with each other how best to screw this Anglo-Saxon and his company.

In Arabic-speaking countries, the benefit of not allowing people to know that you understand what they are saying is different, because Arabs—Moslem Arabs, at any rate—will generally deal honestly with you. I shall say more about what that benefit is when I deal with corruption.

### French Speakers

Francophone monoglots don't have as much to go at as their English-speaking competitors but there's still a lot. Leaving aside Europe (Belgium, Luxembourg, Monaco, Switzerland, France itself) there are plenty of countries around the world where French speakers are welcomed; the majority of the big ones are in Africa but don't overlook Quebec. If you achieve nothing else by turning up there, you'll irritate the Anglos—and to a Frenchman that's a bonus. Right?

### Spanish Speakers

Not much for you in Africa apart from Equatorial Guinea and parts of the north coast, but South America is a goldmine.

### Non-speakers of English, Spanish or French

Learn one of those languages or stay home.

## Passports

Have at least two. Some countries take a long time to issue visas and they are holding your passport all the time they are thinking about it; if you only have one, you can't go anywhere else while you're waiting. It's easy enough in most countries to get a second passport; a letter signed by a director of your company saying who you are, what you do and why you need two passports will do the trick.

## Visas

Some countries allow visitors to obtain entry visas on arrival at the airport or seaport and some don't. You can't apply any intelligent guesswork to this—if you have a US, British or European passport you need to get your visa in advance to visit Australia but not Lebanon, which is probably the opposite of what most people would imagine. Some countries (Suriname is one I pick entirely at random) will grant tourists a visa on arrival but make it rather more difficult for business visitors.

## *Health Certificates*

The one I'm thinking of here is the "Yellow Card", the International Certificate of Vaccination or Prophylaxis; this:

**Yellow Card**

The Yellow Card can only be issued by doctors licensed to do so and the only disease specifically designated by the International Health Regulations (2005) for which proof of vaccination or prophylaxis may be required as a condition of entry to a country is yellow fever. To get a Yellow Card you therefore have to be vaccinated against yellow fever; the card will be good for ten years.

The question of who needs a Yellow Card is not as simple as it may appear—it depends both on where you are going to and where you are coming from. For example, if you fly to South Africa from the US you will not be asked to show your Yellow Card—but an American will need one when he lands there from Kenya or Tanzania (countries considered to harbour yellow fever). Arriving in Ghana, it doesn't matter where you've come from—showing the card is obligatory. A country by country list is published by the World Health Organisation (WHO) and you can find it online here:

www.who.int/ith/chapters/ith2012en_countrylist.pdf

I recommend that you check this publication in connection with any country you plan to visit.

Malaria may not require a Yellow Card of its own but malaria (like yellow fever) is caused by mosquito bites and the WHO website says that 106,820 deaths from malaria were reported in 2011, by 99 countries and territories with ongoing malaria transmission, compared with 30,000 yellow fever deaths—so take malaria seriously. There's no vaccine—if you're going to a malarial area you take medication before you go, while you're there and after you get home. There are different kinds of medication; once upon a time I found simple Artemisinin tablets (available over the counter) effective but the disease is now largely resistant to this so I switched to a widely used prescription drug and it made me psychotic (and no, I am not exaggerating). I now use Malarone; it's more expensive but a legitimate business expense and I have found no side effects with it. That doesn't mean that you won't, of course, so experiment until you find something you're comfortable with.

Then there's Dengue fever, another killer. Many countries that have it don't like to talk about it. I was in Riyadh in April 2014 and read in the local press about Saudi Arabia's success in reducing the recorded cases of Dengue fever. I've been going to Saudi for decades and that was the first I knew it was even a risk there.

## Food

When you travel, you're going to eat. Just as you do when you're not travelling. Obviously. If you're a few thousand miles from home, the food may not be what you're used to. Look around you in the restaurant. Is anyone dying? No? The food isn't poisonous, then. I don't know why it's necessary to say this but the best food to eat in someone else's country is what the locals eat. Okay, okay, I have a favourite restaurant in Shropshire and it's French, so clearly I don't practise what I preach; I don't eat pap in South Africa or hens' feet in China (and cockerels' testicles?—forget it); what I'm really saying is: don't be afraid to eat what you can get—but, sometimes, you may wish you hadn't.

I don't much care for noodles, but in South Korea I've eaten plenty. I'm even less enamoured of kimchi, the Korean national dish which, in its commonest form, consists of fermented cabbage. Every time my Korean hosts ordered kimchi they would say, "You won't like this". I did wonder why, if they knew that, they pressed it on me.

However, kimchi won't kill you. In Turkey once I ate steak tartare and I thought I was going to die. It was four days before that feeling disappeared. Steak tartare is still one of my favourite dishes, but I'm now much more careful about where I eat it. Belgium is always fine—and so is Abu Dhabi, and it's thinking about that that makes me, still, surprised about the Turkish experience because Abu Dhabi is a Moslem state and so is Turkey and cleanliness is such a central part of Islam that you can generally rely on everything connected with your meal, including the hands of the people who prepared it, being spotlessly clean.

You can't do that in India. I love Indian food as served in India but I've been there many times and I don't think I have ever left without an upset stomach. I don't care how expensive and five star the restaurant or hotel is—somewhere in the chain that brings the food to your table, someone hasn't washed his or her hands; and what those hands have also been used for, you don't want to think about.

But the food is delicious, so eat it. Just make sure you pack lots of Loperamide and, if you're stricken, drink water because it's easy to become dehydrated. (Before you get on to the Loperamide, you might like to know what someone in Libya taught me about dealing with an upset stomach. Squeeze the juice from two lemons into a glass and drink it exactly as it is. Don't add water; don't add sugar; drink the lemon juice neat. It's years since I learned that and it's often been the only treatment I needed. Nor have I ever stayed in a hotel that couldn't rustle up a couple of lemons when I asked them to).

## *Freight Forwarders*

Find the best freight forwarders you can. That probably won't mean the cheapest, but choosing a freight forwarder on cost alone is a mistake. Freight forwarders arrange transport from your factory to the customer's country but the good ones do far more than that. They warn you when you are in danger of breaking regulations in the importing country; they manage the process of getting documents certified and legalised; they present documents to the bank under Letters of Credit or where the terms of business are Cash Against Documents.

Some freight forwarders specialise in small areas (I know one who is a whiz on imports to Iraqi Kurdistan, which are generally handled by shipping to Mersin in Turkey and overlanding it from there to Erbil because—and this was already true long before Kurdistan decided to withdraw from Iraq in the aftermath of ISIS—shipments to Umm Qasr, the main Iraqi port, will almost never complete the journey north) and some know how to ship to a continent or two; what you want is people who know your market(s). I've worked with the international giants in this field and some smaller firms. Both can be excellent, but whichever you go for make a point of getting to know the people in your local branch.

## *Harmonised System Codes (HS Codes)*

This is a globally recognised classification system on which Customs tariffs are based. You can find the HS Code for your products here:

www.foreign-trade.com/reference/hscode.htm

Don't give in to requests to quote an incorrect code so that the customer can get a lower rate of import duty—you'll be breaking the law and that is not a good idea.

HS codes should be included on your quotations and invoices.

## *Managing Your Time*

Air fares are expensive and you need to make the best use of them. Don't fly to one place, stay two days and then fly home with a view to flying somewhere else a few days later. Try to coordinate visits to a number of countries at the same time. Typical country combinations I have found effective are:

- Tanzania to Kenya to South Africa

- Dubai to Abu Dhabi (they're only 100 km apart by road) to Oman

- Jeddah to Riyadh to Dammam to Bahrain to Dubai

- Japan to Indonesia to Malaysia

- Belgium to Denmark to Sweden to Germany (all by road from the UK going out on the shuttle through the Channel Tunnel and coming back by ferry from Hook of Holland to Harwich; there's a very nice ferry from Sweden to Germany)

# Chapter 2:
# Things to be aware of
# before you sign up

- You'll spend a lot of time alone.

- In more than half the world's markets, corruption is endemic.

- You do it their way—not yours.

- You have to go there.

- Get the detail right, because you may have a long way to go to fix it.

- Other people's politics are nothing to do with you.

- Beware the (wo)man who knows the President.

- Whatever you've read is probably wrong.

- Almost nowhere is as bad as the media say it is. But, just occasionally…

- The dangers of alcohol.

- Enjoy yourself.

Let's go through those one at a time.

## *You'll spend a lot of time alone*

International salespeople need to be self-reliant and feel comfortable when alone in an unknown country. They should be happy in their own company because that's often all they have.

On the other hand, there may be times when you wish you could get a few hours on your own. In India in particular it's hard to get people to understand that you'd like an evening to yourself—eat dinner in the hotel, attend to emails, write your report on the day's activities, watch some TV/read a book/get an early night. The people you're visiting will not believe you. They will feel they have a duty to entertain you, and they will do it; and it will take time.

What you realise very quickly is that willingness to leave you alone varies according to the importance of family life in that person's country. In some parts of the world—India, much of the Middle East—there is no acceptance that a man's place in the evening is at home with his family and those are the countries where you may have to assert yourself to get any time alone. In the West, hospitality will often be offered but no-one will think any the worse of you when you opt for a night in.

## *Corruption*

This is such an important matter for anyone involved in international sales that it has the whole of Chapter 3 to itself.

## *You do it their way—not yours*

It's fine to be proud of the way they do things in your country and your company. What is not fine is to expect others to do things the same way. Wherever it is that you're planning to sell, find out what their working practices are and adopt them (as long as that doesn't mean breaking the law—see Chapter 3, Corruption). In Chapter 4, Research, I'll look at ways in which you can find answers, but first you need questions. Here is a list, by no means exhaustive, of the things you need to know for each country you are thinking of targeting:

# The International Sales Handbook

1. Just how big is the total market for your products?

2. Who are the big players in your market?

    2.1. As suppliers

    2.2. As customers

3. What general price levels have you been able to ascertain?

4. Do you have something new to offer? Or simply a Me-Too?

5. What government regulations govern the market?

6. Is there a specification or standard you have to meet?

    6.1. Which government department sets it?

    6.2. Who else has a say in what can be sold?

7. What percentage weight does the market give to the following (i.e., how do they balance the competing claims of these factors?):

    7.1. Quality

    7.2. Price

    7.3. Country of Origin

8. What is the rate of import duty for your products? And what will it cost to get them there?

9. Does the Government require pre-inspection for your products? If so, which agencies are authorised to carry out inspections and against what specification does inspection take place?

10. What shipping documents are required?

11. Is there a requirement for invoices and other documents to be:

11.1. Certified by a Chamber of Commerce?

11.2. Legalised by the importing country's Embassy in your country?

12. Can your company sell direct or are you required to:

12.1. Appoint a local agent or distributor?

12.2. Have a local partner?

12.3. Register a legal entity?

13. What is the norm for packaging?

If you're new to international sales, there may be items in that list (pre-inspection, perhaps, or legalisation) that you haven't heard before. Let's go through the points one by one.

## How big is the total market for your products? Who are the big players? What prices are people getting?

I put these questions first because they are potential show-stoppers. Selling to another country is always going to be more expensive than selling in your own. Is there enough money there to justify the expense? There's a lot you can do to find the answers before you get on a plane to find out for yourself—see Chapter 4, Research. Before you do that, take a look at Appendix 1, The Trap of Apparently High Market Price.

## Do you have something new to offer? Or simply a Me-Too?

There's plenty of evidence to say that the first person or company into a new market or launching a new product has an advantage that is not easily taken away. You can compete with this first-comer in one of the following ways:

1. With a better product—something that lasts longer, has additional features, performs better;

2. With a better name in the market;

3. By being cheaper.

Let's look at those. Selling a better product is always the number one choice; I have built my whole career on two mantras:

- A Premium Product at a Premium Price; and

- You can have it good. You can have it cheap. But you can't have both at the same time.

Selling a premium product at a premium price is the route to happiness as a salesperson. However, you can only do it if a premium product is what you have; if it isn't, you are thrown back on the other two choices.

By "a better name in the market," I mean that your company's name is renowned worldwide—3M, IBM, Siemens—but that's academic because, if you work for one of those companies, you don't need this section of the book because whole departments exist in your company to make decisions for you. You may be smaller than that but so pre-eminent in your industry that everyone in your marketplace knows how good you are, but however well-known your company is you may have to spend quite a lot of money on marketing to take a bite out of the entrenched competition unless you are also offering extra features. Is there sufficient margin in your selling price to make this worthwhile? Will that still be true when the competition responds by cutting prices?

And then there's the last resort—undercutting the competition. If selling a premium product at a premium price is the most fun salespeople can have with their clothes on, selling on price is the least enjoyable. Personally, I'd rather be dead, but if you have to do it, you have to do it. But do you have to? Please remember that the alternative to entering a new market by cutting prices is not to enter that market at all; and that may be the more sensible choice.

The thing most likely to go wrong when you try to enter a market by undercutting the established suppliers is that you discover that they have been making higher margins than you thought and will slash them to keep you out. (See Appendix 1). Your options then are limited; in fact, if you are offering a Me-Too with no advantage in quality, reputation or innovation, you only have these:

1. Stay out of the market on the grounds that it simply isn't worth the risk; or

2. Find an agent or distributor to represent you in the market.

I deal with the question of finding an agent or distributor in Chapter 6.

## What government regulations govern the market?

There will be many products for which this is not an issue but, if you sell anything with a safety connotation—if your customers are in the construction, pharmaceutical, machinery or transport markets (among others)—there are almost certainly going to be standards, specifications or other regulations imposed and enforced by the government of the country you are selling to. How you find out what they are is something I deal with in Chapter 4 on Research; for now I'll content myself with this:

When you start out, it will seem sensible to rely on the people to whom you are selling to tell you what the national standard or specification is. And so it will be, more often than not. But you will not be doing this job for long before you realise that some of the people you are dealing with know very little about the market. In Africa, in the Middle East and in South East Asia many of the enquiries you get will come from people and companies who are not in the business but would like to be. They have heard of a big contract—quite often a friend or relative in Government will have told them about it and will have offered to influence corruptly the winning of the contract in return for a share in the profits—and now they need a supplier so that they can bid. A quick search on Google turns up your name and so they email you telling you they want to buy your products and asking for prices. You reply with a couple of simple questions: *Is the standard in their country AASHTO (American) or EN (European)? Has the Government imposed requirements like minimum softening point or warranted shelf life?* and it becomes clear that they don't know. So *you* need to know.

## Who else has a say in what can be sold?

If you sell products for the construction industry, it won't only be the Government that sets the standard. Any sizeable construction project will have a consulting engineer (usually a consultancy company) and a main contractor and, even if you are selling to a relatively small subcontractor, the consulting engineer and the main contractor will both have to agree to the use of your products. To achieve this you will probably need to make what in many places is called a submittal, and that's a very good reason to have a local subcontractor doing it for you unless you have actually set up a branch or subsidiary in the country. Even if you are using a local company they will still need your active support.

Appendix 2 sets out what may be found in a submittal (this example was taken from an actual case in Saudi Arabia). Before you (or your local customer) can prepare a submittal you need to know what it is that you're submitting for. That means you need (at least): a specification of the product(s) the consulting engineer has stipulated should be used; and a bill of quantities, saying how much of each will be needed. You make your submittal to the main contractor, who submits it to the consulting engineer and feeds the result back to you. Appendix 3 shows a typical response to a submittal; the place you need to look first is, helpfully, right after the first heading: Action Codes. What you hope to see is a tick in the first box: *Approved, work may proceed.* Except for the simplest tenders, it is very unusual to get this result first time out—you may find yourself resubmitting two, three or even more times before you get that go-ahead. What we have received in this case is a tick in box three: *Revise and resubmit, work may not proceed.* There follow a series of comments, all of which need to be dealt with before approval can be obtained (the actual response I took this from had three pages of comments; I have shown only one).

To emerge from this process with approval and an order can take some time but it requires more than time; what you need most of all is people on your side who want to get your product approved and that is where the salesmanship comes in. Before you ever get to the submittal stage you need to have sold the subcontractor and main contractor the idea that yours is the product they want to use. If you haven't done that, you're never going to get the order which is your only objective.

I stress this because there are a number of things that go wrong during the submittal/approval process and you need to be well-enough connected to know when they are happening to you. Sometimes a procurement person is already in the pocket of another supplier. That buyer may work for the main contractor or the consulting engineer. If s/he has agreed to accept payment for getting someone else's product approved, there are various things they can do to get in your way. Not passing on the engineer's comments to you is one; not forwarding your replies to the engineer is another. (I can recall quite a number of times when the engineer has told me, "But you never replied to our request for more information" when I know that we did). If you've done the hard work, got to know who it is at each level that deals with your submittal and made follow-up calls on that person yourself or got your customer to do so you are much more likely to know when things are not going as they should.

Winning approval and getting the order doesn't always have to be this complicated. At the time of writing this I have two examples of a much simpler process on my desk; in each case we are where we are because we have already convinced the contractor who will be doing the work that ours is the right product for the job. In the first example, our customer emailed that the engineer on the project for which the customer wanted to use our product had objected that the viscosity was too high. I sent back a letter on our letterhead with a signature and our company stamp (in many countries these are essential for any kind of official communication so, if you don't have a stamp, get one made—and make a JPEG for electronic signing by stamping a sheet of paper, signing over it, scanning the stamped and signed sheet and cropping it to size). The letter said (very politely) that the AASHTO standard the engineer was applying actually applied to a slightly different set of products. It also gave the standard that should be applied. The engineer accepted the letter, the product has been approved and we expect our order daily.

The second example resulted from a rushed response by one of my colleagues. The customer knew he wanted to use our material and he emailed a copy of the specification being used and asked for a Technical Data Sheet that showed our product's compliance with the spec together with a company profile. Now, my colleague was on holiday at the time—but salespeople, unless they're part of a team, don't really have holidays in the way that other people do. You check your emails and, if they need an urgent reply, you find the time to send one. So he did—but he didn't read the spec as closely as he might have and didn't notice three important things: the material was to be applied at a thickness 0.5 mm lower than the data sheet said it should be; the standard being applied was an old British Standard that was replaced several years ago by a European Standard and the data sheet only showed compliance with the current standard; and in some places the product was to be used in a way that was perfectly acceptable but wasn't mentioned on the data sheet.

Because I was the person who had first sold to this customer, he brought me into it with an email that said he was not amused and that, although he valued our relationship and wanted to continue to do business with us, he would go to someone else if we didn't fix things. He also said that he was flying out of the country the following afternoon and wanted to be able to deliver the documents to the project engineer for approval before he left. I spent that evening checking the spec and confirming: that the material could be applied at the lower thickness; that it still met the old British Standard as well as the new European one; and that it could be used in the additional way specified. Then I rewrote the Technical Data Sheet to show all of those things, converted it to a pdf file and sent it—with a company profile and copies of our current ISO certificates—so that it was in his inbox when he got to work the next morning.

All of this is part of meeting the consulting engineer's requirements and getting the order.

## *What percentage weight does the market give to the competing claims of: Quality, Price, and Country of Origin?*

One of the pleasures of selling to Japan and Switzerland is that they love quality and they're prepared to pay for it. If you have a product that is demonstrably better than anything anyone else is selling, they'll want it and they'll expect it to cost more than lesser competitors. If only that were so everywhere.

If you want to hire someone to sell to the Middle East, make sure you don't take someone who thinks price is whatever the customer wants to pay. What you need is a salesperson who has been trained to sell QUALITY. The Middle East is a big place, but in the GCC countries especially (GCC = Gulf Co-operation Council: Bahrain, Kuwait, Qatar, Saudi Arabia, Oman and the United Arab Emirates) the cheapest product sets the price—if you let it.

There's an interesting aspect of human nature here. I have found that Governments in the poorest countries (obviously I don't include Japan and Switzerland in that category) are prepared to pay more for a product than those where money is simply not a problem. Mozambique, for example, is one of the poorest countries in the world and Qatar is, per capita, the richest—but I have found that Mozambique will pay far more than Qatar for road markings, road safety surfacings and other safety systems and similar items. Now let's not get carried away here; part of the reason is that a lot of road financing in Mozambique is paid for by the European Union and similar bodies and spending other people's money is never as difficult as spending your own—but the main reason is that, when you're poor, you know that what you buy has to last and durability is worth paying for. If you're as rich as Qatar, you don't see a problem in paying to have a shoddy job repeated more than once in the time that a single application lasts Mozambique.

There's another side to that, too, which I will cover in Chapter 3 on Corruption. All I'll say for now is that a Government official in a GCC country once said to me, "If your material lasts three times as long, I'll need three times the commission." By "commission" he meant "bribe"; I pretended not to understand.

What you need when you're selling to GCC and other Gulf countries is a determination to get across the message that Quality has to be paid for. Adopt the mantra: You can have it good. You can have it cheap. But you can't have both at the same time. Again and again you will be told that the product they are now using is poor and that yours is the one they want—but when you name the price they will say, "But we can buy it cheaper than that." The "it" they can buy cheaper is the one they have just been complaining about. You will be told quite frankly that you have to meet the cheap price. You must reply every bit as frankly that you can't, and even if you could, you wouldn't. You will find this easier if they see you regularly—see Chapter 4 on You Have to Go There.

## *Import duty and freight*

If you read through Appendix 1 when we talked about How big is the total market for your products? Who are the big players? What prices are people getting? you already understand the importance of this information. All I will add here is that you will sometimes be asked to quote on invoices and other documents a tariff code that you don't think is the correct one for your product. The request comes because the customer can get a lower rate of import duty for the code he wants you to use than he will on the code you believe you should use. If you're tempted, remember that you'll be breaking the law of the country you are selling to. If you're caught, your reward may be gaol. Don't do it.

## *Pre-inspection*

Of all the things that cause grief to the international salesperson, nothing matches pre-inspection. Not even corruption brings this amount of pain.

A number of countries demand that imported goods be inspected before they are shipped. In theory, this is to ensure: that the goods are what you say they are; that you are not shipping something of inferior quality; that the goods meet the importing country's specification; that you are not taking part in a manoeuvre to get money out of the importing country illegally. I did say, "in theory". In practice, many importing countries can feel secure on none of these counts.

It isn't government agencies that inspect your goods; inspection companies are private enterprises. I have nothing against the four main inspection companies (Bureau Veritas, Cotecna, SGS and Intertek), but they can't have inspectors everywhere so sometimes they appoint subcontractors and sometimes the subcontractors use freelances. To do the job effectively, those people need to (a) know something about your industry, and (b) care about doing a good job. Sometimes they do, and all goes smoothly. And sometimes they don't.

Here are some bad things that have happened to me; I'm not naming names because, although all of these stories are true, the people I named would take offence. It isn't a law suit I'm afraid of because the fact that something is true is a good defence against a charge of libel; I've met the people I'm talking about and some of them would be quite capable of taking a machete to me. Nor am I going to name countries, because doing that might make it clear who I'm talking about.

Unimaginable Delay. At the time of writing this I am waiting for an inspection to be carried out on goods ordered for delivery to a country in the Middle East. We had the goods in stock when the order was placed and on the day we received the order we asked for the inspection to be carried out. That was more than four weeks ago; we have chased the people assigned to carry out the inspection several times but we still don't know when it will happen. The customer is getting very restless and is threatening to cancel the order unless we can ship very soon. Twenty days ago, the inspectors told us "our technical team are already assessing the file and we hope to respond by the end of this week." When we heard nothing, we contacted them again (fourteen days ago) and were told, "the file is still being assessed by our technical team." Another ten days went by after which the inspectors asked us to provide full details of our testing methods and laboratory equipment together with photographs. No indication of why they had not asked for these things earlier. We sent them the information they asked for; we are still waiting for an inspection date. (Note added eight weeks after writing this. The order was cancelled because the customer could wait no longer. The inspection company didn't care—they still got their fee and they hadn't actually had to do the work).

Unimaginable ignorance. We had an order to ship goods from our factory in Malaysia to a country in southern Africa which required inspection before shipment. Inspection was delayed by five weeks because the people assigned to carry out the inspection believed that Malaysia was in China and nothing we could say would persuade them that they were wrong.

Nothing to test against. This is an example of how far wrong something can go and no-one really be to blame. We sold $1 million worth of goods for which the importing country had no approved specification. The purchase was approved by the Ministry that would have been responsible for issuing a specification, if one existed. We had previously sold that country quite a lot of other material (for which a specification did exist) and always had to have the goods inspected. I asked whether inspection would be required in this case. Yes, I was told, it would. I pointed out that our previous experience was that inspection for that country involved confirmation by the inspection company that the goods complied with the specification, which in this case did not exist. No problem, said the Ministry; they gave us a letter saying that inspection in this case should be limited to confirming the volume of goods being shipped, and that the invoice amount tallied with our usual market price for those goods. We shipped the goods. When they arrived, the Customs authorities refused to allow them to be cleared because there was no confirmation by the inspection company that the goods met the specification. Our customer showed them the Ministry's letter and was told that that cut no ice—the Ministry in question had no authority to vary Customs regulations, and Customs regulations required confirmation of compliance with specification. Stalemate. The goods sat on the dock and demurrage began to be charged. (Demurrage is a charge that the docks make for space occupied after a certain time). Then we received an advice from the shippers that the goods were approaching the time limit set for uncleared goods and that if they were not cleared soon they would be seized and sold at auction. That wasn't a problem to us because we had sold against a Letter of Credit payable at sight (see Chapter 5) and we had already had our money—but we did feel an obligation to our customer and we did what we could to help him along, including asking our Embassy in the country to see what they could do. They made representations to Customs on our behalf but with no effect. Then one of the Embassy's local staff took our customer for coffee and marked his card for him. I would never let anyone tell me what was said because I must not know (see Chapter 3), but I'm pretty sure it was along the lines of, "Go and see the man whose blocking you and ask how much he wants". Of course (once again, see Chapter 3) I have no idea whether money changed hands but the obstruction ceased and the customer was able to clear the shipment, though he still had to pay the accumulated demurrage which was by no means peanuts.

Some countries manage the inspection business sensibly. We have sold to Saudi Arabia for twenty years and the goods we ship there have to meet the Government specification, but the Saudis content themselves with a report from an independent laboratory (nominated by us and approved by them) certifying that they have tested a sample of our goods and they meet the specification. From time to time (it averages every five years) they will tell our local customer that the certification is getting a little long in the tooth; we get another one done and everyone is happy.

Nigeria, too, goes about things in a rational way. The Standards Organisation of Nigeria (SONCAP) exists to ensure that goods imported into Nigeria meet the minimum requirements of Nigeria Industrial Standards or any other approved international standards; you can find a full account of SONCAP at  http://www.son.gov.ng/son-services/soncap/. If you expect to sell regularly to Nigeria, contact SONCAP and ask for their assistance in obtaining a Certificate of Conformity. Your factory will be inspected and your goods tested, but once you have that Certificate of Conformity everything will be plain sailing. What I like about both the Saudi and the Nigerian testing regimes is that they do not require inspection of every single shipment before it can leave your factory.

You will find a full list of countries requiring some form of pre-inspection here:

http://export.gov/logistics/eg_main_018120.asp.

Your forwarding agent should know what is required for each country they ship to and they should advise you at the same time as they quote a freight rate. If they don't, find another forwarding agent.

John Lynch

## *What does the Government demand from Shipping Documents?*

I deal with this in more detail in Chapter 5 on Incoterms and Terms of Payment. For the purposes of this chapter, what we're concerned with are the requirements of the authorities in the country you are shipping to—specifically, the level of authentication they want to see. There are countries to which all you need to send is an invoice, packing list and a Certificate of Origin saying which country the goods were manufactured in. But some countries are far more demanding than that. You may have to have your documents certified, in which case some body (usually your local Chamber of Commerce) has to certify that your company is who it says it is—certification usually amounts to little more than that. There is a fee, it's quite modest and the best way to handle certification is to get the forwarding agent handling shipment of your goods to do it. Legalisation is more demanding: when an importing country says that documents must be legalised they mean that, after certification, the documents must be sent to their Embassy in your country to be checked and stamped. In some cases they will also insert another step into the process by saying that, after certification and before legalisation, the documents must be certified by a different Chamber of Commerce (e.g., the Arab-German Chamber of Commerce, the Arab-US Chamber of Commerce, the Arab-British Chamber of Commerce). Legalisation carries a higher fee than certification (when you are setting your selling price, be sure to include these additional costs); once again, the best way is to get your forwarding agent to handle everything.

Legalisation can take time—embassies of Middle Eastern countries may take four weeks to stamp your documents and send them back to your local Chamber of Commerce, who will then send them back to your forwarder (or you, if you haven't entrusted a forwarder with the task). There's nothing you can do about this, but you need to bear it in mind when you're booking a truck to take your goods to the dock or the airport. (When I first went to live in an Arab country—many years ago now—I heard the expression "Maybe after tomorrow" in answer to the question, "When will this happen?". I have heard it many times since then, but in my naïve early days I thought, "Okay. Today is Tuesday, so—Thursday." That's not what "Maybe after tomorrow" means. The best translation would be, "It won't be today. It won't be tomorrow. After that, who knows?" That's how it is in the Middle East and, if you can't adapt to it, perhaps you'd better find someone else to sell there.

## Can your company sell direct? And, if they can, should they?

There are a number of things you need to be aware of here. First, some countries have exchange control regulations that will prevent you from being paid unless your customer (a) has an import licence and (b) gets Central Bank approval for the transfer of money before the order is placed. Don't assume either that this applies only to poor countries or that the granting of an import licence automatically includes permission to remit the funds overseas (i.e. to you). It may or it may not and you need to check. If your research (see Chapter 4) tells you that your customer needs an import licence, ask at the very least for the licence number; if you are in any doubt, ask to see a copy.

Then there are the countries that either require or prefer that the goods be imported by an entity that has a registered presence there. If you already have a dealer, distributor or agent that should do the job; otherwise you will find in certain countries that registering a presence may give you an edge. The regional government of Iraqi Kurdistan, for example, looks more kindly on imports from companies who have registered a presence there (they don't have to go so far as to set up a local company). BUT:

If you do decide you need a local company, then in some

countries you can't have control because a local must have 51% ownership AND:

In parts of Southern Africa, and in particular in the Republic of South Africa itself, you have to deal with increasing pressure to advance the interests of historically disadvantaged members of that society. (I'm sorry if you think "historically disadvantaged" is unnecessary political correctness, but it is the accepted form of words). As dissatisfaction grows with progress since the end of apartheid there is a growing demand for Government action to increase the rate of wealth transfers between whites and the rest of the population. This is very much a "Watch This Space" matter; a few years ago companies got away with token appointment of a few black people to nominally management positions (Narrow-Based Black Economic Empowerment) but the move to Broad-Based Black Economic Empowerment is more demanding.

If you want to sell to Government or Government-funded projects, you had better also be aware of growing protectionism. As I write this, the South African economy is in difficulties and the rand is weak, so the desire to replace imported with locally manufactured goods is strong. When a manufacturer approaches Government with the argument, "Why are we importing Product X when we make Product X ourselves?" they are increasingly well received and the fact that locally made Product X may be of poorer quality than your imports may not help you secure the business.

## What is the norm for packaging?

This is probably a more important question for American companies than for almost anyone else because the rest of the world is metric and America isn't. Where American goods tend to be packaged in gallons, pounds and tons, international markets demand litres, kilograms and tonnes. Where American coverage rates will be given in feet, inches and miles, customers overseas want the measurements in centimetres, metres and kilometres. If your Data Sheets show coverage rates in the

# The International Sales Handbook

American measures I strongly recommend producing new ones for export markets showing the figures in their metric equivalents.

There's a further trap when selling from America to English-speaking countries in Africa because places like Nigeria, Ghana, Kenya and South Africa may not understand that the US gallon and the US ton are not the same as the British gallon and the British ton, which they are more used to. A British, or "Imperial", gallon is 20% bigger than a US gallon. A British or Imperial ton is 2,240 pounds; a US ton is only 2,000 pounds. As it happens, a British ton is only 1% larger than a metric tonne and one is for most purposes considered to be the same as the other, but that 240 pound shortfall in the US ton causes problems. When I began to offer an American substitute to customers in Africa who had previously lapped up our British-made product I stressed to the US factory that the tonnes in question consisted of 2,240 pounds. They promised that shipments would be adjusted accordingly—but they weren't, and we ended up shipping additional pallets after the original orders had been filled, to make up the difference. The customers hated it and gave me an ultimatum: go back to shipping the British product or lose the business.

If that sort of change isn't possible, as in most cases it won't be, make your quotations as easy as possible to relate to the competition so that your offer can be properly evaluated. Recently I quoted a company in the European Union for products which I can only supply packaged in pails containing 5 US gallons each. I knew that the competition would be quoting litres, and I knew that the customer was accustomed to thinking in litres and not in gallons (and certainly not in short US gallons), so I wrote my quotation like this:

2,000 US gallons @ US$12.55 ex works USA (=$3.31 per litre)

You also need to know what packaging requirements—apart from volume—the customer and the importing country's government have. If they say they want in tins something you normally supply in paper sacks, don't ignore the difference. By all means ask if they will accept sacks instead of tins, but if the answer is that they won't then you'll have to calculate the cost of making the change, look at the likely volume of business and decide whether you still want to quote. If you do, word your quotation with care. Here's an example of what can go wrong:

A government Invitation to Tender invited bids for 54 tonnes of material to be supplied in tin cans instead of the paper sacks the manufacturer normally used. To comply, the manufacturer would have to install new packaging equipment. They costed this and decided that, if they added $4.26 per kilogramme, they would break even over the whole 54 tonnes and still have the new equipment at the end of it. In their bid (with which they had to put up a bank guarantee for 10% of the total value), they failed to stipulate that it was conditional on receiving an order for the full 54 tonnes. They won the tender, but were told that a reassessment of requirements meant: that only 30 tonnes in total would be ordered; that the first order would be for ten tonnes; and that fulfilment of the first order did not mean that they would receive the following two orders of ten tonnes each. Investing in the new equipment was not now a paying proposition—but turning it down meant their bank guarantee would be called in. I repeat: word your quotation with care.

Look also at the symbols and wording that are required to be on the packaging and make sure you can comply.

## *You have to go there, get it right first time*

I'm a great believer in Skype—it allows me to have long conversations at no cost with people all over the world. I've also put in the hours on conference calls. Those are both great aids to communication but they don't take the place of actual visits because, in many parts of the world, customers will only deal with suppliers they see regularly in the flesh. I make sure I'm on the ball with our Saudi customer by Skyping weekly with the General Manager, but I also visit him four times a year. In fact, at the start of each year one of the first things that goes into my new diary is the projected start and end dates for Ramadan—because visiting Saudi Arabia during Ramadan is a waste of time and I want to make sure my visits are scheduled in the most productive way.

## Get it right, because it's a long way to go to fix it

Yes, it should be obvious, but so often it doesn't seem to be. You're in Harlow New Town, you send something to Leicester and when it gets there it's faulty. Okay, it shouldn't have happened and you've probably given yourself an objection you'll have to overcome but the two towns are only a hundred miles apart and an engineer can be there in two hours. It's a problem but it isn't the end of the world. You're in Harlow New Town, you send something to Benin and when it gets there it's faulty. Now you do have a problem, because as far as Benin is concerned, Harlow New Town really is the end of the world. Can you fix the problem on the spot? Okay, if you're there and you can do that you might even win brownie points by showing them how easy a fault is to correct. If you can't, though, what are your options? Ask a forwarder to pick the dud up and ship it back to you while you send out another one? Face it: you shouldn't have got into this position in the first place. Avoiding it, though, is not just about you, the salesperson; effective international selling requires that the whole company gets involved and everyone knows her or his part in making it work.

## Other people's politics are nothing to do with you

Mark Twain said that "nothing so liberalizes a man and expands the kindly instincts that nature put in him as travel and contact with many kinds of people." I wish it were true. In fact, travel causes friction because so many people go to new places determined to explain to Johnny Foreigner what he is doing wrong. If you're a missionary, carry on (but don't expect sympathy when your head is boiling in a pot). If you're interested in selling something, keep your mouth shut. The values and ideas you grew up taking for granted are not shared by everyone. I know you think the advantages of Western-style democracy, equality between the sexes and advancement on merit alone are so obvious that all you have to do is explain how they work and people will fall over themselves to get these glories for their own societies. You may be astonished that so many of the people you meet don't agree. You're there to win orders, not arguments, so leave politics alone (and that goes double for religion).

## *Beware the (wo)man who knows the President*

Over the past forty years I have lost count of the number of people I've met who had the power to open doors that would otherwise remain closed to me. Their friend was sister/brother to the man/woman who was married to the President's sister/brother-in-law. When the ruler wanted to recharge his batteries with a few days in the desert, just him and a trusted confidant and three hundred security men with Kalashnikovs, the confidant was the person you're speaking to. His/her mother cast the runes/read the tea leaves/spread the Tarot cards before every important decision the President made. You're not going to sell a thing without this person's assistance. And you know you can trust her/him because s/he isn't asking for a penny as a retainer—all s/he wants is a letter saying that s/he is your appointed representative in the country in question, and a contract to pay commission on sales. If s/he doesn't do the job, you don't have to pay a penny—that's how confident of success s/he is. It's a no-brainer. Right?

Well, yes. It is. But not in the way s/he means.

The first question to ask yourself is: how involved is the President likely to be in deciding whether it's your products or someone else's that get the nod? Do you sell nuclear submarines? Warplanes? If so, the President probably is involved—but if those are your products you work for a company that already has close links with the country in question, and you've got your own government doing everything it can to get the decision to go your way.

If you sell almost anything else, cultivating the (wo)man who knows the President is a waste of time. This person knows everyone—but "everyone" does not include the people who set the specification, the people who carry out the evaluation or the people who place the orders. It does not, for example, include the procurement clerk who has to sign the order and who is simply not going to do so, whatever anyone says, until he receives the payment he considers his due (see Chapter 3, Corruption).

The drawback to signing that contract to pay commission on sales can be in the way the contract is worded. My advice, however, is that you should almost never sign a contract of this sort.

## Whatever you've read is probably wrong

I'm going to begin this section with a complete change of subject.

As R J Lynch, I write historical fiction. It fits well with the rest of my life; constant changes of time zone, frequently across the International Date Line, destroyed my internal clock years ago so I find myself awake thousands of miles from home at three in the morning and that's when I get up and write. In researching for my James Blakiston Series of crime novels set in County Durham in the 1760s I spent some time in the Durham Archives. Now, everyone who knows anything about the subject knows—and I stress that; they *know*—that workhouses did not come to the north-east of England till the 1830s. That is in every text book on the subject I've ever come across; it's taught in universities; it's a fact. But go back to the primary documents, as I did when I sat in the Archives and read Ryton parish's Account Book of Overseers, including Assessments of

Poor Rate, Receipts and Memoranda (Durham Registry Office, EP/Ryt 7/1). Woodside Poor House is there, starting in 1759, and the poor were given the choice of entering it or going without assistance. What everyone knew to be true was, in fact, wrong.

It's my view that that is usually the case—that, if everyone knows something, the something everyone knows is not true.

I exaggerate, of course. But I will stand by this rewriting of the heading to this section: Don't believe what you read or what someone tells you until you've satisfied yourself that it's true. And that applies especially to what you read in the newspapers, hear on the radio or watch on television. Journalists don't (necessarily) lie deliberately, but they don't usually get to spend much time in a place, the people they talk to are self-selecting (and quite often do lie deliberately), their articles and pieces to camera are almost always abbreviated and the result is that the picture you get is, at best, partial.

You should also bear in mind that journalists have bosses who want something to excite their customers. "Everything's calm; nothing to see here" won't sell newspapers. So, things get exaggerated. I was actually in the Hotel Corinthia in Tripoli, Libya when armed militiamen came in and took the Prime Minister away. If you believe the Western media, Tripoli was mayhem that day—a cockpit of strife; a maelstrom of violence and fear. The reality was that children went to school, shops opened, business was conducted as usual and everything was calm—but, as I say, that doesn't sell newspapers.

The best indicator of whether a place is safe will come from the people there. During the 2013 upheavals in Egypt I had a trip planned to Cairo. Three days before I was due to leave my customer called me: "This is not a good time to be in Cairo. Please postpone your visit." So I did. And in July 2014, when a customer in Benghazi got on a plane with his family and flew unexpectedly to Heathrow, I accepted that this time what the press was saying was in fact true: Benghazi was dangerous.

All of which brings me to:

## *Almost nowhere is as bad as the media say it is. But, just occasionally...*

Nigeria, Iraq, South Africa, Syria, Libya—all countries I have visited in the last few years. Which is the most dangerous place I've been during that time? Moss Side in Manchester.

The press gives all those places a bad name but the reality is that the thing you most have to fear is: wrong place, wrong time. In all of those countries I just mentioned the majority of people want the same things. A safe environment where they can live their lives without fear of violence or disease. A roof over their heads and a job to go to. Food for their families and education for their children. Freedom from arbitrary arrest and the ability to get the things they need without having to pay bribes.

Those are probably the things you want, too. And that's the point. Most of the people you will meet are very like you and they bear you no ill will.

Most of the people.

When you travel in places you've been told are dangerous, conduct yourself as you would if you were at home, treat the people you meet as friendly, but be aware that trouble may not be far away. Develop the habit of watching people. Those young men leaning against the wall—are they watching you? If they start to move, are they coming in your direction? Are you closer to your car than they are? That veiled woman who just put her bag on the ground. Is she about to walk away and leave it? Are you catching on people's faces looks you'd rather not see? And is this taxi driver the one you expected to pick you up?

You'll develop a set of rules for your own protection. The first one on the list, at least in Africa, should be: never get into a car unless you were expecting it, you know who the driver is, you know where it's going and someone else knows where you are and who is taking you there. If, as it occasionally will, that rule proves unenforceable, take a picture of the car's licence plate on your mobile phone, email it to someone at your office with a message saying "If I don't arrive where I'm going, this is the car I'm getting into" and tell the driver what you've done.

The best way to find a trustworthy driver in a country you've never visited is to ask your hotel to pick you up at the airport. If you like the driver they send, take his card and stick with him from then on. When you need to visit a customer who isn't sending a car for you, text "your" driver and ask if he can take you there and wait for you till you're done. If he can't, ask him to recommend someone who can. Next time you plan to visit the country, text the driver in advance and ask him to collect you from the airport.

Understand that, in some countries, the high rate you pay for a hotel room is not for luxury, it's for safety. In Lagos, Nigeria, I have two hotels I stay in; both charge five star hotel rates but neither is better than three stars—what I'm paying for is the knowledge that, once I'm inside that fence, no-one is going to get at me. Good hotels in Nairobi will usually have at least one security guard on each floor. They're not there for show. In Saudi Arabia, Libya and a lot of other places, hotel driveways will be laid out so that no-one can drive a car laden with explosives into the hotel and all vehicles will be stopped at the gate while the boot (trunk if you're reading this in America) is searched and a detector is run under the car. You may also have to pass through airport- style security to get into the hotel (or into a government office).

Try not to go outside the hotel with wallet, credit cards or other valuables. Remember, though, that the safes in hotel rooms aren't that safe; if you want to know how easily they can be cracked, ring the front desk and tell them you've locked yours and forgotten the code. Then watch the person who comes to open it for you and see how long it takes. (It won't be long). The best approach—leave as much as you can at home.

If you're outside on your own in a number of African countries, watch out for the guy who speaks to you and knows which hotel you're staying in and even which room. He says he works there; maybe he even claims to be the one who showed you to your room. He's temporarily short of cash but if you will help him with a loan he'll pay you back as soon as he returns to work. Maybe he says he has to visit his mother, who is ill and needs his help; maybe he even suggests you get into his car so that you can see that what he says is true. Don't give him any money and don't get into the car. He didn't show you to your room; he doesn't work in the hotel; he got a call from the guy on the desk when you left the hotel and they will share whatever he is able to get out of you.

If your luck runs out and you are held up, don't fight it. Some years ago, I was on my way from my Lagos hotel to the airport to catch a flight to Dubai. It wasn't my usual driver but he had been assigned by the hotel and I felt safe. We were stopped at a road block and a policeman stuck his head (and a gun) into my face and demanded money. I shrugged and answered (in German) that I didn't understand. He looked disappointed (he didn't speak German) and shrugged but let us drive away. As we did so, the driver said, 'That was a very stupid thing to do.'

Of course he was right. I had let anger influence my actions. I was no stranger to Lagos and I had known as we drove that we were not taking the obvious route to the airport—we were on a little-used road and as soon as I saw the roadblock and the policeman I knew it was a set-up and the driver was in on it. (Was the copper even a real policeman? I have no idea). I got away with it—but what would have happened if the driver had said, 'He isn't German. He's English'? I could have been in a lot of trouble.

The usual advice is: If they want your car, give it to them. If they want money, give it to them. And hope they let you walk away. And supress the normal wish to trust people you've known for a while. All the evidence says that, if you're kidnapped or murdered, it's more likely than not to be with the assistance of someone you know—possibly even think of as a friend. That was true when girls in Northern Ireland were encouraging squaddies to fall in love with them and trust them so that they could be taken somewhere to be murdered and it's true in Iraq where the man who promises to guide you and keep you safe is the one who has promised to deliver you to a group that will hold you hostage for two years and then film your beheading.

## The dangers of alcohol

I like a drink as much as the next man, as long as the next man isn't Peter O'Toole, and I don't want to be thought a prig but one of the best pieces of advice I was given at the very start of my career was: don't drink when you're on your own. Over the years I've watched a number of careers end before they should have because alcohol dulled both ambition and performance. I'd now add something to that don't drink alone rule: when you're on the road, only drink alcohol when you're entertaining (or being entertained by) customers. One of the easiest things in our business is to go to the bar after (or—worse—before) dinner, get into conversation with your peers (which is a good thing to do because you never know what you might learn) and then start matching them, vodka & tonic for vodka & tonic. You'll lose your sharpness, you won't do the things you should be doing (like writing reports on the meetings you had that day and planning your presentations for tomorrow) and your performance will suffer. Think of alcohol as a treat for the evening you arrive home.

## Enjoy Yourself

Looking back at some of the things I've written, it seems like a lot of warnings. They're all meant—but international sales has given me enormous pleasure over the years. Let it do the same for you. Don't be so focused on looking out for danger and not giving offence to people whose religion or politics are different from yours that you can't enjoy the fun side of travel and the pleasure of seeing new places and meeting interesting people.

# Chapter 3:
# Corruption

Unless you sell to a very restricted number of countries—the UK, Scandinavia, the USA, Australia, New Zealand, Canada and Germany—you're going to encounter corruption. I don't mean that those countries are entirely free of corruption—they're not—but it's so common in the rest of the world that you will not do business without becoming aware of it. So you'd better read this chapter.

Personally, I've lived with the knowledge of corruption for so long that the thought of it simply doesn't bother me. Corruption is said to be undesirable on ethical grounds and because it distorts competition. Well, other people's ethics are their business, not mine and as for distorting competition—isn't that a salesperson's job?

When I was Sales Manager for Africa and the Middle East I used to say that, excluding Saudi Arabia where business is somewhat more honest, no contract worth more than $500 was signed anywhere on my patch without money changing hands and I don't believe anything has changed. What has changed, though, is the legal framework and we need to be aware of it.

In theory, the anti-bribery legislation that has appeared around the world produces a more level playing field. In fact, the reverse is true because (a) not all countries have introduced a bribery law and (b) not all of those that have, enforce it. In 1997, 38 countries (they don't include China, India or Russia so whether you're buying or selling that's three of the world's largest markets excluded) signed up to the OECD Convention—to give it its full name, the Convention on Combating Bribery of Foreign Public Officials in International

Business Transactions. Since then, some individual countries have introduced their own laws. The UK's Bribery Act came into force in 2011 and the USA has the Foreign Corrupt Practices Act. You can expect both of those to be rigorously enforced. Most European countries have added articles to their Criminal Codes and in some cases the legislation is a joke.

In the Czech Republic, for example, the Criminal Code provides for up to twelve years in prison, fines, forfeiture of assets (and not just criminally acquired assets) and disqualification from ever holding office again. The definition of a bribe is all-embracing: "offering, giving, requesting or accepting (directly or indirectly) in the public or private sector an unauthorised benefit resulting in a direct material enrichment or other advantage which is obtained or is intended to be obtained by the bribed person or another person with his/her agreement, and to which that person has no right." Ferocious, *n'est ce pas?* Enough to put any naughty person off? Well, go to Prague, apply for a licence to set up business there, refuse to bribe the official and see how far you get.

But get the British Government on your back and you may as well enter a monastery. (On second thoughts, emigrate— they'll find you in the monastery. The monks will dob you in for fear of being accused of conspiracy).

Let's be clear about what we mean by corruption, because we should distinguish between two very different categories:

- Corrupt government officials;

- Corrupt company employees.

There are a few countries where both groups of people are on the take; in one fabulously wealthy GCC country every single person you deal with, government or commercial, will want to be paid off. (Why don't I name this place? Because I haven't retired yet, I still go there from time to time and their judiciary is not above jailing people for insulting the country; the fact that you spoke the truth and can prove it is no defence.

It is a perfect example of the sad fact that the more you have, the more you want). Generally speaking, though, cupidity lies on one side or the other. In Italy, for example, you won't go far wrong if you assume that every single government official is bent while management of the companies you deal with is simply trying to stay afloat in a venal world; in Saudi Arabia, on the other hand, officials are generally Saudi citizens and honest—the graft comes from procurement staff, most of whom are on low salaries but intend, when they return home to the sub-continent, to be a lot better off than when they arrived (and most of them achieve it).

I'll add that, when the amounts involved are very large, people come looking for money who wouldn't normally soil their hands. If you're in the defence industry or selling major transportation or mobile phone installations you'll deal with royalty (or whatever equates to royalty in the country in question). For more on this see *Big deals can present a very different picture* below.

## Channelling the host country's money into someone's pocket

A true story from a North African country in 1966: a western contractor is working on a project for a government ministry. Each week he submits an invoice for the work done during the previous seven days. Let's say that the value of the work for that week is 500,000 riyals; the contractor raises an invoice for 550,000 riyals, attaches a cheque for 50,000 riyals and hands invoice and cheque to the junior civil servant whose job is to receive requests for payment. The civil servant knows how to distribute the 50,000 riyals; 25,000 (let us say) will go to the Minister and three riyals to the old man who sits by the door and makes chai while everyone in between gets his or her correct share. A little later, the contractor receives payment of 550,000 riyals and everyone is happy.

So what has happened here? The contractor has paid

nothing—he has acted as a conduit enabling government employees to get the job done while also transferring some extra money from the government's coffers to their own pockets, the going rate in that country at that time being 10%.

As I said, that happened in 1966 (and I know it did, because I was involved). It isn't quite like that now—and yet the same thing happens. These days, the 10% (though in the country I speak of it's now a lot more than that) is paid as commission to an agent. What happens is this:

- The salesperson makes the sale to the end customer, ensuring that the agent has at least some form of involvement

- The salesperson tells the agent, "When the dust has settled, this is the amount that has to remain in our bank account"

- The agent talks to the customer and then tells the salesperson, "Issue your invoice for $x$", $x$ being the sum the salesperson's company needs to have in its account at the end of the process together with a percentage, which will be the agent's commission

- When the invoice is paid, the agent invoices the salesperson's company for the commission, which the agent distributes as agreed with the customer; it is essential that the salesperson takes no interest in this part of the process and is not informed how the commission is distributed because a salesperson who has knowingly participated in a corrupt transaction may face prosecution in her/his own country.

## Buying business

Some time ago, a middle-ranking manager in the Public Works Department of a small but stunningly wealthy island in the Arabian Gulf agreed that the product of a well-established

Western company could be evaluated for use on the island. Evaluation would take the form of a practical test—the manufacturer would supply material free of charge and its performance would be monitored for six months after application. The catch, from the manufacturer's point of view, was in the choice of who would apply the material. The manager would not accept the manufacturer's own crew—application must be by a local contractor who had worked for the PWD before. The contractor told the manufacturer he wanted US$50,000 to carry out the application. The manufacturer said it should cost US$5,000 at most and the contractor said, "You pay me $50,000 or your material will fail."

I can tell you that in that case the material was never supplied, the $50,000 was never paid and the material was never evaluated. I'm in a position to say that because I was the salesman involved and I made the decision not to pay the bribe—because that's what it would have been. I didn't make that decision on ethical grounds; I made it because recovering the money through long term sales was a doubtful proposition. We were one of six manufacturers being invited to submit material for trial; I had no doubt that all six were being asked for $50,000 (I know for sure that two of them were, because they're friends of mine); there was no commitment that final approval would be given to any one of us and I didn't doubt that further donations would be requested when orders were eventually placed. It was not, as I say, an ethics-based decision—I made it because (a) the amount we were being asked to pay was too high in relation to the profit if we won the business and (b) there was a 5 to 1 possibility that we would pay that money and not in the end receive the order. (If you wonder why the PWD's manager was so helpful to a local contractor, the answer is simple—the contractor would expect to split these $50,000 payments with the manager 50/50).

A different problem raised itself when the Ministry of Transport in a country where I have done a lot of business wanted to replace the product they were currently using, which failed too frequently. We showed in a series of tests that our product was easily the best on the market and could be expected not just to last but to go on performing for at least seven years. This caused the officials involved real difficulty. Of course seven years was infinitely preferable to the nine months or less they were currently getting—and, over those seven years, the cost of our product would be at most half, and probably less than that, of the cost of continually replacing the inferior stuff they were using. Anywhere in Western Europe the decision would have been a no-brainer—but this was the Middle East. Every time that inferior material was used, Ministry personnel received from the contractor five per cent of the contract price as bribes. If they allowed a switch to our material, the contractor would have to increase the price by nearly fifty per cent to allow the men from the Ministry to maintain their income. And that, they decided, would be too obvious. They stuck with the poor quality stuff. Last time I checked they were still using it.

## *Paying to make something happen*

When the Bribery Act 2010 came into effect in the UK, we invited a solicitor specialising in this field to give a presentation at our Sales Conference on what we could and could not do. After we'd listened to what she had to say, I asked if I could give an example of what actually happened. This is the example I gave:

"I'm in, let's say, Alexandria. We have three containers on the docks and our Egyptian customer needs to get them out of there—if he doesn't start work on his contract soon, he'll face penalty charges. We walk into the docks office and present the documents that should allow us to clear the goods. The clerk says, 'These documents are not in order.' I know, and he knows, that there's nothing wrong with the documents; I also know that he knows that I know that he knows … etc. I take a US$20 bill from my pocket (I keep a supply of them about me for just this purpose), put it on the counter (keeping my hand on it) and say, 'I wonder if there's anything we can do about that?' The clerk eyes it and then stamps the documents (to say they are all right and the containers can be driven away) and puts them on the counter right beside my hand. I pick up the documents and the $20 disappears into the clerk's pocket. We leave the office and call the transport company to move the containers to the customer's yard."

The lawyer said, "You can no longer do that."

I'm afraid I laughed.

The contractor on the Island of Unimaginable Wealth and the clerk in the Alexandria docks office are not in any way comparable. Every one of the island's citizens (there are only a few hundred thousand) is very rich; the place is a perfect example (as I said above) of the fact that the more you have, the more you want. A tiny minority of Egyptians are quite astonishingly wealthy—the huge majority have nothing. When you meet the Operations Director of an Egyptian customer of significant size, try to remember that his salary probably has the buying power of a power tool rental depot manager in Madrid. You wonder why his salesman is driving a small, old car that's falling to pieces? Because that's all he can afford. So how much do you think the clerk on the docks takes home? Most Egyptian workers rely on tips, and that's how the clerk will regard the $20 he pretty well forced you to give him—as a tip. If they don't get tips, they may struggle to eat.

Allow me a little diversion here. I arrived at Cairo International Airport and got onto the bus operated by the hotel where I usually stay. The other passenger on the bus was a young Japanese businessman. As you may know, the Japanese don't tip. They regard tips as an insulting suggestion that the person they are tipping is inadequately paid. However, an Egyptian bus driver knows he is inadequately paid and he won't feel insulted if you add a little extra. We arrived at the hotel and I gave the driver $2—enough to feed his family for a couple of days. The Japanese gave him nothing. As we walked to

Reception, the driver skipped after the Japanese, asking if everything was okay. Yes, yes, all was fine. I said. "Tip him." "What?" "Tip him!" "Oh. No." Okay, have it your way. So we walked into the hotel; the driver followed us, speaking to the receptionists in Arabic which the Japanese did not understand; my receptionist said, "Welcome back, Mister John; we've upgraded you to a room in the Tower, no extra charge"; and the Japanese's receptionist said, "I'm sorry, sir, I can't find your booking." Okay, she would find him a room eventually because they wouldn't want to lose the money but she'd make him wait and I might well be showered and ordering dinner before he got to his room. The lesson: in Egypt, tip.

## Dealing with Procurement staff

If you're in the Gulf, chances are that a lot of the buyers are not local—they've been brought in from other, poorer, countries. They aren't paid very much but they're determined to go home at the end of their contract with a nice pot of savings and, by and large, they achieve that. Where does the money come from? It comes from the companies who sell to their employers. From you, in fact.

This one is awkward. You've jumped through all the hoops the target company officially puts in your way. You've got your product approved by the responsible manager or committee. You've submitted your ISO certificates, Technical Data Sheets and Safety Data Sheets and you have whatever government approvals you need. So you're done, right? Well, no. You still need the order—the piece of paper that says, "Deliver this and we'll pay you"—and that comes from Procurement. In theory, you don't need their approval. In practice, you probably do.

The reason it's difficult is that you can't dress it up. The "tip" to the clerk in Alexandria Dock? A business expense, reclaimed monthly with your other cash disbursements. Padding your invoice and paying the difference to the staff? A commission for helping you win the order. But this—paying someone in the buying department to hand over the order he's been instructed by his own management to issue? That's a bribe and you can't pretend it's anything else. How you deal with it will depend on what country you are working from. If you're French, you can take the standard French line which is that the law is for other people. German salespeople working for German companies will probably feel okay about paying because, while business in Germany is about as clean as it's possible to be, Germans take a sensible approach to other people's ways—they know someone will pay the bribe or the order won't be placed and they see no reason why their own workforce should lose their jobs because expatriate clerks in the Gulf are less scrupulous. If you're British or American, though, and not already established in the Gulf, you're going to have to let this order go.

Why do I say, "not already established in the Gulf"? Because when you have a partner there, the partner will make these arrangements for you and will meet your need not to know that any bribe has been paid. But don't let that rush you into appointing a distributor/agent/partner—see the section in Chapter 2 on Beware the (wo)man who knows the President.

## *Taking money to influence a decision*

If a salesperson has the power to influence a decision—to decide who becomes his/her company's distributor; to choose which contractor gets the valuable contract; to overlook failure to achieve a contractual term—someone, sometime, somewhere is going to offer the salesperson money. One day, it will happen to you. If you're tempted, I'd just like you to know that someone will know—someone always knows. Once you've accepted a bribe—because that's what you'd be doing—your behaviour changes, and so does the behaviour of the people who paid you. People see those changes and they know what you've done. Your colleagues will know, your boss will know, your competitors will know—and, perhaps worst of all, you will know.

I'm not just talking about money, by the way. Anything that has a price (I've been offered a woman before now) should ring the alarm bells.

All you need to remember is to say how grateful you are for the offer but, "I can't accept any payment from anyone but the company that employs me."

None of this should prevent you from accepting modest entertainment. It's fine to accept a ticket to a sporting event, as long as you're paying your own air fare and hotel bills. I've enjoyed rugby and cricket matches in the southern hemisphere, but only when I was there on business anyway and my company was paying for everything but the sporting ticket. It's also okay to be taken for a nice meal, though I have always protected myself by ensuring that I return that particular favour.

## *Big deals can present a very different picture*

Most bribes are small beer. Things change when the contract is worth millions of pounds, dollars or euros because then people who wouldn't normally be attracted by the small sums on offer see a chance to make themselves financially secure for life and you're in a very different game. Please try to remember that the chance of being exposed rises exponentially and you're risking a heavy fine, the expropriation of your personal assets, public ignominy and jail time. And you may have company in prison because your actions might result in your Managing Director being there with you. Ask how s/he feels about that possibility before you do anything you shouldn't.

## *Entertaining your customers*

Passage of the Bribery Act in the UK sparked all sorts of horror stories. Unfortunately, some of them turned out to be true but some were nonsense. It was said, for example, that if you had a box at Old Trafford you would no longer be able to invite customers there unless every one of your competitors also had such a box because that would mean you were enjoying an advantage that they could not afford. We now know—or, at least, we think we know, because it has not been tested in the courts—that it's still fine to invite customers to watch a match and to feed them while they're there.

It's also okay to take visitors for a meal.

And, if they're visiting your factory and they need to spend two days there, it's probably all right to pay their hotel bills for those two days.

What you need to be able to show is that what you have paid for was proportionate, reasonable and necessary. If they're going to be in your country for a week, only pay for their hotel accommodation for the time they are actually spending with you. And don't under any circumstances pay their air fares.

## *Use the legislation to explain what you can and can't do*

You receive an email from a customer. Quite a big customer and one you don't want to lose. The email tells you that two of the customer's staff are coming to your country with three people from his country's government, they'll be there for a week and you are to buy the plane tickets and pay the hotel bills for all five visitors.

No, this is not a ridiculous invented scenario; this is an email I received from a customer in the Middle East. I would always have refused the demand because I don't like being taken either for granted or for a fool, but saying "No" is now much easier: all I had to do in this case was to explain that we have a new Bribery Act in the UK, that it tells us what we can and can't do, and that one of the things we can't do is what we were being asked to do in this case. Conversation over.

# Chapter 4:
# Research

In this chapter I will take the questions raised in Chapter 2 and suggest ways to find answers. It's mostly very obvious—so why do I see so many people attempting to sell in markets they know nothing about without first trying to establish some basic facts? Obviously, your preferred search engine will help you find a lot of the answers; let's look at some additional sources.

## *Local knowledge is always best*

Let's say you want to know what the law in Libya says about foreign companies doing business there. Type into Google the words "International law firms in Libya" and a number of names will turn up. Clyde & Co is one, and I'm happy to mention them here because I've used them successfully in the past. Now, Clyde & Co have offices in London, New York, San Francisco, Toronto, Sydney, Paris, Madrid—so all you have to do is tell your local Clyde & Co office what you want to know and they'll contact their people in Tripoli and get a report for you. Nice and simple and you didn't have to leave the comfort zone of home to get what you wanted— but probably not the best way you could have handled this.

My experience is that gathering knowledge remotely is never as good as going there and talking to the people on the ground. The man or woman who lives there and deals with the country every day will come up with things in conversation that would never get into a written report. You can ask questions and get immediate answers (without paying an additional fee). So, if you go to Tripoli and make an arrangement to meet a Clyde & Co lawyer there, I can promise that you will leave that meeting more fully informed than if you handle it all from your own country.

John Lynch

## *Bear in mind the vested interest of whoever you're talking to*

Saudi Arabia is a valuable market for me and I've noticed in recent years that the competition from US companies, once fierce, has declined. Some large American companies that I regarded as significant threats simply don't go to Saudi Arabia any longer. In one case, when I asked why, I was told, "It's a corporate decision, and not just for Saudi. We don't go to the Middle East, period. Too dangerous." When I looked at the US Government website http://www.travel.state.gov/ I realised why: on its page on Saudi Arabia it says, "The Department of State urges U.S. citizens to carefully consider the risks of traveling to Saudi Arabia. The security climate in Saudi Arabia continues to improve, despite an attack of unknown motivation on two German Embassy officials in Awamiyah in the Eastern Province in January 2014. The last major terrorist attack against foreign nationals occurred in 2007, but security threats are ongoing and terrorist groups, some affiliated with al-Qaida, may target both Saudi and Western interests."

I'm sorry, America, but this is ridiculously over the top. I spend a lot of time in Saudi Arabia and the reality is that it's no more dangerous—and probably safer—than Miami or Buffalo, NY. And that was also true seven years ago in 2007, when that "major terrorist attack" you refer to happened. Yes, I'm more careful in Eastern Province than I am in Jeddah—but I go there. The one area I have tried to stay away from is the Southern Border area—but now that Saudi relations with Yemen are improving, even that is not a no-go region.

The UK Government advice on https://www.gov.uk/foreign-travel-advice/ is more restrained: "There is a risk of tension in the Saudi-Yemen border area over illegal traffic in people and goods. Take great care in all areas close to the Saudi-Yemen border." That's all they say about Saudi Arabia and, yes, I agree with it.

The point I am making is this. In the next section I'm going to be talking about your own Government as a source of information. It's a good one. However, helping their nationals to do business abroad is only one of their interests; another (and potentially more important to them) is avoiding problems with their local opposite numbers. One of those problems is the one that arises when a visitor goes missing in a foreign country and her/his Embassy has to try to get her/him back unharmed. Sometimes you have to approach their advice with caution.

Another and perhaps more sensible source of information on how safe it is to go to a particular country is security companies operating there. Unlike the Embassies, they have a vested interest in getting you to go there because, if no-one visits, they have no customers and no revenue. On the other hand, they have a very strong interest in making sure no harm comes to you while you're there. Sticking with Libya so that we can see the same topic from various angles, I looked at the weekly Situation Report on Libya from Salamanca Risk Management—a company I have used while in the country. About Tripoli they say only that you should avoid flights whose arrival time "requires passengers to be driven up the Airport Road late at night, when the risk of roadside robbery is significantly elevated." About Benghazi they are more cautious, saying that "international business engagement with the city [is] difficult, though not impossible; there are expatriate visitors making the trip. However, all travel to Benghazi must only be undertaken with robust and methodical risk mitigation measures applied. This does not necessarily mean that travel can only take place with heavy security presence; profile is the key to security planning in Benghazi as it is in the rest of the country, with light-footed operations achieving the greatest success."

## *What information does your Government provide?*

Most developed countries understand that helping companies to sell abroad is part of their responsibility and good for their economy. Google "Help for Exporters" and you should find a link to what's available in your country—there isn't room in this book to list all the government departments in the world but the USA website is

http://export.gov

and in the UK it's UK Trade and Investment (UKTI) at

www.ukti.gov.uk

Approach the UKTI site in the same spirit of adventure as you would Hampton Court Maze, because one is no easier to negotiate than the other. Contact them and tell them what business you are in and what you want to know. At the very least they should be able to tell you who is active in the sale of products like yours and what sales volumes are like; you may well get more, including invitations to meet likely prospects when you're in the country.

When you do visit a new country it can be helpful to contact (in advance) the Commercial Attaché at your country's embassy and ask for a meeting. Several years ago I made such an appointment at the British Embassy in Nairobi; I was treated to some very nice sandwiches and the best cup of tea I'd had since leaving home and I really thought that that was all I was going to get out of the visit but, when I was in my hotel room, I got a call inviting me to return to the embassy three days later to meet three key players in my marketplace. You simply don't know in advance how helpful they are going to be—so try it and find out.

Government help can be very valuable but it can be patchy; a great deal depends on the background and experience of the person you make contact with. Some are very good and some aren't—so don't restrict your searches to what your Government offers.

## *Who are your main competitors?*

Look at their websites. Do they have pages on their overseas distributors? On projects they have been/are involved in?

## What sort of customers do you sell to?

Google that kind of customer in the country you are targeting. Contact the names you find, tell them what you do/make/sell and ask if you can meet them while you are there.

## Databases for sale

There are companies that sell access to project databases and you may find there information on tenders you could bid for. This has never worked for me but I know people who say they have succeeded with it.

## Your own website

Assuming that your website makes it easy to contact you (and if it doesn't, why not?) you will hear by phone, email or letter from people who are interested in buying from you or in representing you. Don't appoint an agent or representative easily, but this is an opportunity to ask them to tell you all they know about the market they want to interest you in.

## Exhibitions

It's possible to spend a lot of money on exhibitions—building the stand, renting the space, paying for flights, hotel rooms and meals for your people. I can't count the number of these things I've attended over the years; I don't think a single one ever paid for itself in business subsequently won. After you've been in a territory for a couple of years you should be confident that you know all of the decision-makers and call on them regularly so you don't need to meet them at exhibitions. I know the standard concern: "If we don't exhibit, they'll think we've dropped out of the market". I also know the best response: give a seminar or seminars at or close to the time the exhibition is being held. That way, you let people know that you are still there and you focus your attention and spending only on the people you want to see, because you control the invitations.

However, this chapter is about research and I will

acknowledge one time when exhibitions may be useful in introducing you to your potential customers and your potential customers to you. That time is when you are new in that territory, so that you don't yet know and call on all of the decision-makers.

## Trade Missions

Trade missions are sponsored (and usually subsidised) by your own government. Typically, they arrange exhibitions at which you can take a stand, or simply be there to talk to people. The local embassy's commercial staff get involved, there will usually be a reception at which all sorts of people you might otherwise never meet turn up and you will often be asked, once you have booked your place, what sort of people you would like to meet if it can be arranged. And it often can be arranged, because the embassy usually has more clout than you do. All that, and your air fares and hotel bills are usually lower than they would be if you organised the trip yourself—and, if the mission is in a place where security is questionable, you'll often be safer than you would be if you went alone. I have found these events well worth the time and money invested in them and I recommend them.

## Places not to look for information

I'm talking about banks and large consultancy companies in your own country.

Let's take banks first. There's some wonderful advertising that shows people all over the world and says, in effect, "You don't understand what makes these people tick—but we do." Well, I've had some experience of those banks who know the best ways to deal with people from other lands and other cultures—and they don't. Or, if they do, they're no good at passing the information on, which is just as bad. Nor does the fact that they have branches in those countries seem to make any difference. I'm not going to go on about this because I don't want to invite a lawsuit, but I will offer this: treat your bank's advice with extreme caution and only follow it if it agrees with what you hear elsewhere.

As for the big consulting firms, I've seen very large sums of money spent with no apparent benefit. I'm sure they have people who've been where you want to sell and I'm sure they have masses of boiler-plate text on their hard disks, but the person who pulls it all together for you will be not long out of university or articles and have as much useful experience as your post-boy.

Oh—and be cautious about the advice you get at the golf club. The newly appointed COO of a FTSE 100 company once talked to me about doing business in Turkey—a country I know quite well. What he was telling me bore no resemblance to my own experience and I was not surprised to learn that he himself had never done business there; listening to what he had been told convinced me that his informant hadn't, either. People do talk a lot of rubbish sometimes—so don't ignore any advice you get, but find a way to verify it. Go back to Chapter 2 and the section in which I wrote: Don't believe what you read or what someone tells you until you've satisfied yourself that it's true.

# Chapter 5:
# Incoterms and Terms of Payment

This chapter is about getting paid. There can't be a salesperson anywhere who hasn't been told: "The sale is only complete when you've been paid." That's also true when you're selling to the guy next door, of course, but export sales can throw up problems you don't find at home. As someone said to me many years ago, "So what are you going to do? Sue me? In Malaysia? Good luck."

## *Incoterms*

Incoterms have been set since the 1930s by the International Chamber of Commerce; the latest update is Incoterms 2010. Incoterms decide how the costs of getting the goods into the buyer's hands are split between seller and buyer. The most frequently met, at least in my experience, are EXW, FOB and CIF but here is the complete list:

## EXW

Ex Works. The seller makes the goods available, usually at the seller's business premises, and the buyer arranges to pick them up. All freight and insurance costs are born by the buyer, who also pays the cost of clearing them from the dock or airport where they arrive in his country and pays the import duty. The place where the goods can be collected usually appears after EXW (so, for example, if your factory is in Glasgow you might quote a price as *£1,000 ex works Glasgow*).

## DDP

Delivered Duty Paid. I am putting this immediately after EXW because DDP is the exact opposite of EXW and everything else falls at some point on the line between these two. DDP means that the seller takes on all costs involved in getting the goods all the way to the buyer, including import duties. The name of the place where the goods will be delivered usually appears after DDP.

As I said, those are the extremes, but DDP is unusual and EXW is very common. I'm going to list the rest in descending order of importance—that is, from the ones you're most likely to encounter to the ones most people will rarely see. Before I do, two points you should bear in mind if you are ever asked to sell DDP:

1. Someone has to clear the goods through Customs, get them on a truck or other suitable conveyance and deliver them to the customer. Do you have an agent locally who can do that? If not, it could be terribly expensive.

2. You need to be very clear on the customer's credit-worthiness to use DDP, because you are going to deliver the goods direct into his hands and if he can't pay you (or decides not to) you're in a very difficult position.

## CIF

Cost, Insurance and Freight. The seller is responsible for all costs until the goods reach the seaport or airport that is the final destination.

## CFR

Cost and Freight. Very similar to CIF except that insurance is paid for by the buyer. It's reasonably common for buyers to arrange their own insurance, but if a customer asks you to sell CFR then unless you know the buyer well you should make sure insurance really is in place—if it isn't, and there's a partial or total loss while the goods are in transit, you may find it difficult to obtain payment. Ownership of the goods does not pass from seller to buyer until they have reached the destination port or airport.

## FOB

Free on Board. The seller delivers the goods on board a ship nominated by the buyer at the named port of shipment. The risk of loss of, or damage to, the goods passes to the buyer when the goods are on board the vessel, and the buyer bears all costs from that moment onwards.

## FAS

Free Alongside Ship. Similar to FOB except that the goods don't actually get onto the vessel. The seller undertakes to deliver to a quay, barge or airport loading bay and responsibility for the goods passes to the buyer at that point.

I have never sold FAS and I have used DDP only in cases where the customer was a Government ministry or department, no duty was payable and I had written confirmation of that. If you've been told there will be no import duty, and then you ship DDP and duty is charged, you can get badly burned.

The following categories exist but I recommend that you only consider them when asked by the customer—don't offer them yourself when you quote. You won't be asked for these terms often because they are rarely used—most exporters will find that 95% of their sales are EXW, FOB or CIF.

## FCA

Free Carrier. The seller delivers the goods to someone nominated by the buyer (usually the carrier) at the seller's premises or another named place. FCA is relatively unusual but if you're involved with it be sure to specify clearly the exact point where delivery will take place, as that is where the risk passes to the buyer who becomes responsible from then on for insurance.

## CPT

Carriage Paid To. The seller pays for carriage of the goods to an agreed place of shipment in the seller's country. The buyer arranges (and pays for) freight, export clearance in the exporting country and Import clearance in the importing country. Think of this as being like FAS but where you are not delivering to a port or airport.

## CIP

Carriage and Insurance Paid To. Really, this is the intermodal (i.e. containerised) version of CIF and it should therefore be very common, but in fact CIF is the expression almost invariably used for shipment in containers.

## DAT

Delivered at Terminal. The equivalent of CIF for intermodal shipments though, in practice, the term CIF is used almost exclusively. The seller's responsibility ends when the goods, once unloaded from the arriving means of transport, are placed at the disposal of the buyer at a named terminal at the named port or place of destination. "Terminal" includes a place, whether covered or not, such as a quay, warehouse, container yard or road, rail or air cargo terminal. The seller bears all risks involved in bringing the goods to and unloading them at the terminal at the named port or place of destination.

## DAP

Delivered at Place. The seller's responsibility ends when the goods are placed at the disposal of the buyer on the arriving means of transport ready for unloading at the named place of destination. The seller bears all risks involved in bringing the goods to the named place.

## *Currency*

Domestic sales take place in a single currency, but when you export you have to decide what currency to sell and invoice in.

One of the considerations is certainty: currencies go up and down against each other and if you can sell and get paid in your own currency you are spared the risk of a reduction in your profit—or even the possibility of making a loss—that you would face if your currency strengthened after you had agreed the deal but before you were paid. On the other hand, you would also miss out on the windfall profit if your currency became weaker during that period.

Generally speaking, the buyer is in the driving seat when deciding which currency is to be used because the seller wants the order and the buyer has alternatives. That is mitigated to some extent by the fact that many countries with weak currencies have accepted over the years that they must deal in stronger, internationally traded currencies; chief among those are the US Dollar, the British Pound and the Euro. I have sold huge amounts over the years to South Africa and Nigeria but I have never been asked to sell there in Rands or Naira—it's always either the Pound or the Dollar. On the other hand, if a British company is selling to a customer in the Eurozone then I strongly recommend invoicing in euros.

If a customer insists on being invoiced in a currency in which you don't have an account and don't want to or can't set one up, it doesn't have to be a problem. We, a British company, had bank accounts in pounds, US dollars and euros. During 2014 I took an order for 23 million Jamaican dollars. (That isn't as impressive as it would have been had the dollars been US—it equates to about US$200,000). We issued the invoice in Jamaican dollars and didn't say anything on the invoice about the value in any other currency; in our own books we entered the transaction as £110,000. The bank details on the invoice were for our British pound account. When the money arrived the bank converted it from Jamaican dollars to British pounds (charging a commission and making a profit on the exchange, naturally). The amount that ended up in our account was more than £110,000 because we had done what you should do in this situation—added something to the selling price to guard against the possibility of the invoiced currency weakening against the pound.

You can do that with any currency, but it's a good idea to learn what you can about the currency before you do. The Emirati Dirham, for example, to take a currency completely at random, is pegged to the US dollar so knowing what you expect the dollar to do will tell you how the dirham is likely to behave.

When you're invoicing in a currency not your own, take into account the credit period you're giving. If the customer is going to pay you tomorrow you probably don't have a problem. If he has six months to pay then, first, you need to build into your price the interest your bank will charge you on that money for that period and, second, you should add something more for the risk of currency fluctuations that go against you.

## *Quotations*

If you want an order you have to tell the customer what the goods are going to cost and you do that by sending a quotation. There may be a series of emails or conversations discussing the price but a final, formal quotation is necessary to make sure all terms of the transaction have been covered. The quotation should include, at the least:

- Precise details of the goods including your Product Code, description and HS Code (see Chapter 1)

- The terms of payment (see next section)

- The number of units and the weight per unit

- The price per unit and, as an extension, the total price per product

- The Incoterms code signifying who is responsible for shipping and to where

- Unless the sale is ex works, the cost of freight and, if applicable, insurance

- Any additional costs including legalisation of documents

- The nature of packaging to be used

- Any other terms that have been negotiated for this transaction

- The date on which the quotation will cease to be valid

- A statement that acceptance of the quotation will be subject to your standard terms and conditions (it will be helpful if these are printed on the back of the quotation)

It is most convenient if the standard layout of a quotation is the same as the layout of order confirmations and invoices. Either a word processor or a spreadsheet can be used (though price extensions and totals are easier on a spreadsheet) but the quotation should be converted into a pdf file before sending. Do this with Adobe Acrobat Pro so that you can password protect the pdf document and prevent it from being altered. Don't send the original spreadsheet because that would allow your customer to see the figures you used in your price calculation.

When you send the quotation, send with it a product brochure, technical data sheet and material safety data sheet. Where the product is to be used in some process in the importing country (for example, sales of building materials to a contractor) I find it useful to send a document describing best practice in the application of the product; this eliminates a lot of argument when the contractor has not followed your instructions on how the product should be applied.

## Terms of Payment

Giving credit always contains an element of risk, whether the sales are export or domestic. However, not giving credit can also be risky because it could make the difference between winning and not winning the order. Some markets understand that their customers will always have to pay cash with order; some expect credit as a matter of course.

Before you go far down this road, you have to consider what will happen if you've given credit and have difficulty collecting payment. What sort of contract have you established with the buyer?

## The Contract

You should have standard terms and conditions on which you trade. Every time you set up a new account you should send a copy of your standard terms and conditions and ask them to acknowledge receipt. They almost never will, so when you invoice them the invoice should make it clear that the order is accepted subject to your standard terms and conditions. If any special terms have been agreed—on packaging, for example— those special terms should be stated on the invoice.

## Cash with Order and Sight Letters of Credit

The safest way to ensure you are paid on time is to get the money before you ship the goods and you do that by asking for cash with order. Send a pro forma invoice and hold on to the goods until you see the money in your account.

Your customer's bank will produce a SWIFT Advice showing that the money has been transferred and you can ask your customer to email you a copy; that will give you a lot of confidence but see Chapter 8 What can go wrong? for an example of how a forged SWIFT Advice can get you into trouble; if you're in any doubt at all, wait till your bank tells you the money is actually there. When you receive the SWIFT Advice, check the bank and account details to make sure they are as they should be.

A Letter of Credit (L/C) payable at sight is the next best thing to Cash With Order and, for those who don't know, I had better go through what a L/C is. First, let me make clear that what you should ask for is not just a Letter of Credit but an Irrevocable Documentary Letter of Credit Confirmed by a Prime Bank in your country Payable at Sight.

The first thing to understand about L/Cs is that they are not agreements to exchange money for goods—they're agreements to exchange money for documents. If the documents are correct you'll be paid—even if, when the customer examines the goods, he finds they are not what he expected. What the documents are is dealt with further on in this chapter, but in essence they give the buyer title to the goods. Here's how it works. The customer takes your pro forma invoice to the customer's bank ("the issuing bank") and asks for a L/C to be issued in your favour. The issuing bank sends the L/C to a correspondent bank in your country—you would like it to be your bank, because that makes life easier and reduces the charges, but that can only happen if your bank and the customer's bank have a correspondent relationship. The issuing bank undertakes, provided the conditions in the L/C are met, to pay you the prescribed amount. The bank in your country (the Advising Bank) then confirms (for a fee) the L/C—it says that, if you comply with the terms of the L/C, it will ensure that you get your money.

The benefits of L/Cs will be clear—you have a guarantee that you will be paid and the customer has a guarantee that he will get the goods he wants. If only life were that simple.

Tell the customer that, before the L/C is issued, you want to see a draft. Examine it closely, get your Finance people to examine it and send it to your forwarder for their comments. The copy you first receive is more likely than not to contain conditions that you cannot agree with and they will have to be changed.

L/Cs are governed by a document issued by the International Chamber of Commerce known as Uniform

Customs and Practice for Documentary Credits. I suggest you get a copy and keep it by you. Here are some of the things you need to check when you see the copy L/C, but if I listed every anomaly I've seen in forty years this would be a very long chapter—so make sure you examine every detail and make sure that everything that should be there is there, and that there is nothing there that could cause you difficulty. This matters because, if you don't comply with the terms of the L/C, the advising bank is likely to send the documents to the issuing bank on a Cash Against Documents basis (see below) and you will no longer have the protection of the L/C.

## Latest Shipment Date

There are two dates you have to concern yourself with and this is the first (the other being the expiry date). The L/C will show the latest date by which shipment can take place. Can you meet that target? Are you sure? If everything that could go wrong does go wrong, will you still be able to ship by the stipulated latest date? If you're not absolutely certain, then ask for the Latest Shipment Date to be changed. What if you've booked space on a vessel, you get the goods to the port in plenty of time but the ship doesn't have room for your container and leaves it in the port to be picked up by the next vessel—which isn't for fourteen days? (Can that happen? Oh, yes. Shipping companies overbook as regularly as hotels and airlines—and for the same reason, which is that they almost always get last minute cancellations; but sometimes those cancellations don't happen. Or your shipment is being picked up in Liverpool, but before it gets there the vessel is loading in Rotterdam—and the shipping company is offered extra last-minute cargo from Rotterdam. You think they'll turn it away on the grounds that accepting it means they can't take yours, which they have contracted to take? I wish I shared your faith in the ethics of shipping companies. They know you don't have an alternative route for your goods so they know your container will still be there when they call again in two weeks. The problems you suffer as a consequence are just that—your problems and not theirs).

And be clear what is meant by "shipment". It is unlikely that you will be deemed to have shipped when the goods have left your factory or warehouse—normally, shipment date will mean either the day the goods get onto the ship or aircraft or even the day the ship sails—but make sure you know which is intended in the L/C you are looking at.

## Partial Shipments Not Permitted

This condition will appear in pretty well every L/C you ever look at and, unless your shipment consists of a single pallet, you almost always have to get it changed so that the L/C as finally issued reads "Partial Shipments Allowed". Go back to that last section, where I talk about the problems shipping companies can cause you. Okay, you're sending three containers and you're confident they will all leave your factory together because all the material is in stock and the trucks are booked—so not being allowed partial shipments won't matter. But what happens if the vessel only has room for two of your containers and the third is left till next sailing? Now you've been forced into making a partial shipment and you're not complying with the terms of the L/C. Trust me: the fact that it isn't your fault will cut no ice at all.

## Expiry Date

The expiry date is the date by which all documents required under the L/C must be in the hands of the issuing bank. When you look at the expiry date on the draft L/C you will, of course, ask yourself whether you believe you can get all documents there by the given date—but please make sure you are in full possession of the facts. You yourselves will be raising the packing lists and invoices, so when those are ready is under your own control. But is legalisation required? (See Chapter 2) It can take three weeks or more to get the documents back from the importing country's embassy, and before they can even go there they have to be certified by the Chamber of Commerce. When you're calculating whether the expiry date is far enough away, do these sums and remember that the legalisation process can't even start until the shipping company has issued the Bills of Lading, which it will normally do three days after the vessel has sailed. And if part or all of your shipment was held back because of an over-booked vessel, this may all be happening two weeks or even more later than you expected. Does the expiry date still look okay when you take this into account?

## Transhipment Not Allowed

If you own the shipping company you are probably safe in letting this stand. If not, not. Exporters have no control over what shipping companies do and, even if they give you a schedule that shows the vessel going directly from Exporting Port A to Importing Port B, there is no guarantee that it will. In ninety-nine per cent of cases, yes—but lawyers get rich at the expense of the rest of us in that 1% of unexpected developments.

## Letters of Credit Not At Sight

Everything above deals with Sight L/Cs. It's years since I last dealt with a Letter of Credit payable at anything other than sight, but they do exist. If you agree to accept a Letter of Credit payable at 30, 60 or 90 days then you are giving the customer credit for that period of time and you should factor the interest into your price calculation.

## Cash Against Documents

When you agree with your customer that your terms of payment will be Cash Against Documents, the sequence of events is this:

- You ship the goods to the consignee

- When you have all the shipping documents, you give them to your bank with instructions that they are to be handed to the consignee in return for the amount of money stated on the invoice

- Your bank sends the documents to its correspondent bank in the importing country. It is a bonus if this is also your customer's bank, but there is no certainty about that—if your bank and your customer's bank do not have a correspondent relationship there is a risk in sending the documents directly to your customer's bank

- The bank in the importing country collects the money from your customer and hands over the documents in return. The customer is now free to take delivery of the goods.

Cash Against Documents works well and I have used it a lot without any problems. That does not mean that nothing can go wrong; as always, it is a matter of Know Your Customer.

The most obvious thing that can go wrong is that, when the goods arrive, the customer cannot pay for them. This can't happen with Cash With Order or a Letter of Credit and it highlights one of the main differences between sales in your own country and export sales. When you ship goods to another country, it is not as easy to recover them as it might be at home. They won't—unless you are the victim of fraud—have passed into the possession of the customer because the documents that would give title to them are still with the bank. Instead, they will sit on the dock. I've already talked about demurrage, which will soon start to be payable, and many port authorities will add fines to the demurrage charges. Worst of all, if the goods remain unclaimed and the charges and fines unpaid for long enough they can be seized by the authorities and sold at auction. It's unlikely that the amount paid will be enough to cover your costs, let alone pay for the goods and give you your profit on the deal—the authorities in some countries will arrange for purchase at auction to be for the amount due in fines and demurrage and the exporter is left with a total loss. A good freight forwarder will warn you before you reach the point where your goods are to be seized and suggest that you pay the outstanding fines and remove the goods.

## Open Credit

By "open credit" I mean that you send the customer the shipping documents that will allow the goods to be cleared and either used or sold and agree to give the customer a set period—thirty days, sixty days, ninety days, whatever—in which to pay you.

In this case, there are two things you need to be careful about:

- Be absolutely clear when the thirty days, sixty days or whatever begins to run. Is it thirty days from date of invoice? From shipment of goods? From arrival of goods in customer's warehouse? The due date will be very different in these three cases

- Police your terms carefully and watch out for one abuse in particular. "Payment due sixty days from date of invoice" means what it says—it does not mean "I'll pay you when my customer pays me," but that is what you will often face. Your business is selling goods. You are not a bank. The customer should have enough working capital to be able to meet normal trading requirements; if not, you made a mistake in granting him credit.

## Combinations of Payment Terms

It's quite common to offer payment terms which are a combination of Cash With Order and some other payment method. Examples:

- 20% Cash with Order; Balance by Cash Against Documents

- 50% Cash with Order; Balance sixty days from invoice date.

## *Credit Insurers*

There are private companies who insure sellers against loss if a customer fails to pay, and there are government agencies— Export Credit Guarantee Department (ECGD) in the UK; Compagnie Française d'Assurance pour le Commerce Extérieur (Coface) in France; Export Import Bank (Eximbank) in the US; most developed countries have them.

I'm not a great fan of credit insurance. The bigger private credit insurance companies maintain databases of information about companies all round the world—how they pay, how profitable they are, whether they've experienced financial difficulties. They can do a good job for you in providing reports and guidance on what level of credit might be reasonable for a company, although their information is frequently out of date. They're less useful when it comes to paying out to cover a loss because they will have a very clear process you need to go through; it is easy to overlook some of the stages and thereby render this invoice uninsured and they will usually want you to take steps against a customer before you're ready to jeopardise the long term relationship in that way. Credit insurers are like any other insurance company— they see their business as taking in money through premiums, not paying out against claims.

Maybe the best way, and certainly my preference, would be to pay private insurers for a report on a company you are thinking of extending credit to, but not entering into a credit loss insurance policy. My present company's Finance Manager maintains that banks are a better source of credit information than insurers because their records are generally more up to date; she may well be right.

Credit insurers can still be useful, though, because even if you don't have credit insurance there may be times when you want to say you do. This has worked for me a few times. If Finance Department says, "No credit for this customer" (and that is a Finance decision and not one Sales are qualified to make) it can be a bit of a downer. Your company has made a negative decision and the customer is entitled not to like it. But if you say, "Look, we're governed by our Finance people and our Finance people are ruled by the credit insurers. I don't know what our credit insurers' problem is because they don't tell us but they say they won't cover us if we give you credit and there's nothing I can do to change that. Even the Managing Director can't change it," then the personal element is taken away and they're much more likely to accept what you say and agree to do business on some other basis. And you can use that formula—say those words—even when, in fact, you don't have credit insurance and the decision was made by your company alone.

## Shipping Documents

I'm including shipping documents in this chapter because they are an integral part of the process of getting paid. To find out what documents are required for exports to any particular country, Google "Documents required for import into…" followed by the name of the country you have in mind. This will tell you everything you need to know about all the documents you need to send. (Note that you google documents for imports and not exports—if you type exports you may find what you need to do to export from that country, not bring goods into it).

I've just googled Documents required for import into Nigeria and got this website:

www.customs.gov.ng/Guidelines/Destination_Inspection/guidelines .php

One of the things that website tells me, which is useful for an exporter to know, is that the importer—that is, the consignee of the goods, who will usually be your customer—has to obtain a Form M and the Form M number has to be on the invoice. A Form M is issued by authorised Nigerian banks which should tell you that it is less an import licence than an approval to pay and it will specify whether or not approval is given to pay in foreign currency. This is vital information for the exporter so before you ship the goods make sure your customer has been issued with a Form M that authorises foreign currency payment and ask for the number. Note, though, that your customer's application for an M number must be accompanied by your pro forma invoice.

The website tells me that the following documents are required when you ship goods into Nigeria:

- Combined Certificate of Value and Origin (CCVO) containing the following details in addition to those on the pro-forma invoice:

- e-Form "M" number

- Adequate description of goods

- Port of destination (and this has to be the *actual* port; Lagos Port is really a complex of separate ports and you must find out from the shipping company which one will be the destination of your goods and name it

- Shipment identification, date of shipment, country of origin, country of supply

- Packing List

- Shipped/ Clean on Board Bill of Lading/Airway bill/Way bill/Road Way bill

- Manufacturer's Certificate of production, which shall state standards and where it is not applicable, the Phytosanitary Certificate or Chemical Analysis Report should be made available

- Laboratory test certificates where applicable

From time to time your documents may include all manner of unusual things, but the ones I have just listed are standard.

## Bills of Lading and Air Waybills

It's worth noting here that the term "Bill of Lading" (B/L) has two meanings in American usage but only one in most of the rest of the world. In most places, a Bill of Lading shows that goods have been shipped on board a vessel (an Air Waybill does the same for goods loaded onto an aircraft for shipment by air freight). That's the kind of Bill of Lading I'm talking about here and perhaps we should think of it as an Ocean Bill of Lading to distinguish it from the other American usage in which a Bill of Lading means the receipt given by a trucker to say that the goods have been loaded for road transport.

Three days after your goods are shipped on board, the shipping company should issue a set of On Board Bills of Lading. What you need to see is clean B/Ls because a foul B/L indicates that the goods were received on board in a damaged condition and that is going to cause you all sorts of trouble, so make sure the packaging is in good shape when it leaves you and is suitable for purpose—robust enough to withstand handling on the way to the port and the journey by sea. It's regularly said that a B/L is a document of title and it is—but only if it's an original, transferable B/L. The set the shipper issues will include both original and copy B/Ls and copy B/Ls are useful because they demonstrate what has been shipped without giving the right to take possession of the goods. (That is what a document of title is—it gives the holder the right to take delivery of the goods).

People become blasé about Bills of Lading. Don't. When you get a new set examine it closely. It will list what has been taken on board—the number of containers if containers are used; otherwise the number of packages or pallets; a general description of the goods; the weight and dimensions. Make sure that these details match your own packing lists because, if they don't, then:

- It could be that some of the shipment is missing; *and*

- The Customs officers at the receiving port will want an explanation of any discrepancies, partly because it's their job to make sure that what is imported into their country is what is supposed to be imported into their country and partly—in some countries—because the existence of a discrepancy creates an opportunity to prise a payment out of the importer in exchange for turning a blind eye.

The B/L should also show that freight has been paid. (If freight is being paid by the consignee, the B/L won't come to you in the first place so, if for example your terms of business with this customer are FOB and not on open credit, make sure you've been paid before the goods get onto the vessel. If you don't, and the shipping company collects the freight charge from the consignee and gives the B/Ls in return, you have lost control of the goods without having been paid).

In at least two African countries that I have experience of, a neat little scam operates. The freight has been paid by the shipper and the B/L says so, but when the goods arrive your customer rings you to say that the shipper's local agent is refusing to release the goods "because the freight has not been paid". The first couple of times this happens, you may think it's a mistake by the agent but it isn't—not if by "mistake" we mean that the agent doesn't know what s/he is doing. S/he knows only too well—this is fraud; a straightforward attempt to get some extra money out of the importer (who will then try to recover it from you). The quickest way to deal with this is to get the shipping company to instruct the local agent to release the goods immediately.

A last point about Bills of Lading concerns the method of release. Increasingly, the B/L is being circumvented in the clearance process and shipping companies are asking the exporter's permission to release the goods without presentation of the B/Ls. You will hear various expressions for this—Telex Release, Express Release and Local Release are three that are common. In this case the shipping company issues non-negotiable B/Ls only, because they do not act as documents of title and documents of title are not required when you're releasing the goods without them. Usually it will be fine to authorise release without the B/Ls, but:

- Always get the consignee's approval first; some people don't like it and neither do some countries

- Are you being paid for this sale by Letter of Credit? What does the L/C say? If it asks for negotiable B/Ls (and it will), tell the shipping company that you're sorry but you must have negotiable B/Ls.

## *Invoices*

You already sell in your own country, so you already raise invoices. You can't usually use the same invoices for export sales. Check the information you downloaded from the website after you googled Documents required for import and make sure you haven't omitted anything that is required.

If you have accounts in different currencies, make sure that the account details on the invoice are for the account in the currency you have invoiced in; if, for example, you invoice in US$s but the account details on the invoice are for a Sterling account, when the bank receives the dollars it will convert them into pounds before crediting your account and you will pay commission and bear the exchange loss (and if you then want the money transferred into your dollar account they will make those charges again). You think your bank has enough nous to see that a dollar receipt should go into your dollar account and not the one it has been remitted to? Dream on.

Don't imagine that, once your bank receives a payment with your company's name on it but without the rest of the account details, they will look around to see what account it should go to and then put it there—they may do that but in my experience they are more likely to hold onto the money for five days and then send it back where it came from saying they can't apply it. If you know the money should be in your account but the bank says it hasn't arrived, get on their back and stay there until they find it. Banks—including the largest and most prestigious—lose other people's money all the time.

Bear in mind that invoices may need to be legalised—see Chapter 2.

## Certificate of Origin, or Combined Certificate of Value and Origin

A Certificate of Origin (CofO) says where the goods were made, not where they are being shipped from. It is signed by you, the exporter, and certified by your local Chamber of Commerce. As with invoices, it may also need to be legalised. If you're in the European Union you can use a European CofO (Form EUR1) unless the sale is to an Arab League country because then you have to have the CofO certified by the Arab Chamber of Commerce in your country after your local chamber has finished with it. By the Arab Chamber of Commerce in your country I mean the Arab-British Chamber of Commerce, the Arab-German Chamber of Commerce and so on, and they won't accept EUR1—it has to be your national CofO.

Everything to do with export trade attracts fraudsters and the origin of goods is no exception. If you are the manufacturer you know where your goods were made, but if your business is distribution I suggest you verify the information you're given because if you misrepresent the country of manufacture, however unwittingly, you will be held responsible.

## *Packing Lists*

You should always include a packing list because I know of no country where they are not required. The packing list should match the invoice and the Bills of Lading; if there are any discrepancies between these three documents your customer will have difficulty getting the goods through Customs. Packing lists are detailed; they should include all of the following:

- Name, contact details and physical address (PO Boxes are not enough) of the exporter and the consignee. This business of PO Boxes can be troublesome; many countries don't have street addresses in the way that, say, the UK or America does

- Gross weight (the weight of the goods plus all packaging, pallets, etc); tare weight (the weight of the packaging without contents); and net weight (the weight of the goods only)

- Nature and specification of the goods being shipped

- Type of packaging

- Dimensions of each package

- Number of pallets, drums, cartons or whatever

- Contents of each unit of packaging

- Package markings

- The number and date of the relevant invoice

- The consignee's purchase order number. (You may not always have a purchase order number, in which case use something that relates to the correspondence between you)

- The name of the carrier

- The Bill of Lading or Air Waybill number

I know this is a lot and some of it is fiddly but it is important to get the packing list right if you are not to cause your customer grief and perhaps cause delays in release in the importing country leading to demurrage charges and penalties.

I come back to the fact that export sales and domestic sales are two different things, and the biggest difference is in the regulations you have to comply with in the importing country. Here is one simple example. Some time ago, I arranged the sale of some material to Kenya from a factory in Texas. Most of the sale was paint but there were also some glass beads. The factory manager did what he usually did when shipping to, say, Oklahoma and put the sacks of beads in empty paint pails "to keep them safe". If he had said so on the packing list, and put labels on the relevant pails saying that they contained glass beads, all might have been well but he didn't. The packing list said that the paint was in 5 gallon metal pails and the beads were in hessian sacks. Kenyan Customs opened the container in Mombasa, saw lots of pails but no sacks, closed the container again and refused to allow the goods to be cleared. It cost the importer a serious number of Kenyan shillings in bribes before he finally got his consignment. The moral? It doesn't matter how things are done in your country—what matters is what the importing country requires.

## Certificates

You will have to comply with whatever requirements the importing country has for products like yours; these may include laboratory test results, statements of compliance with a given standard, your own company's ISO9001 and ISO14001 certificates—the list is almost endless.

# Chapter 6:
# Finding Local
# Representation

## *Customers and agents*

You can't do business in any country (including your own) without at least one customer there. That may be all you need, and it may be all it's wise to have. If you want to do large scale, long term business, though, sooner or later you're going to need a stronger relationship with someone. I recommend later rather than sooner, for reasons set out in the next section.

Something I've noticed on, for example, the US Government's web pages, designed to help would-be exporters, runs like this: U.S. companies do not need to visit [insert name of country] to find an agent. The U.S. Commercial Service can help U.S. companies find the right partner through the International Partner Search (IPS) service. Well, yes. There's no harm in letting the U.S. Commercial Service put forward a few names—but you do need to go there, whatever the website says.

## *Don't rush into it*

You get an email from a man in a country you've never dealt with—let's say it's South Africa. He's seen your website, your products are exactly what his company is looking for; please quote for a 20 ft container load, delivered to Durban. You ask your forwarder for a sea freight quotation from your factory door to Durban dockside. The customer wants to be invoiced in US dollars so you put together a quotation (see Chapter 5) specifying Cash with Order and email it together with a product brochure, technical data sheet and material safety data sheet.

There's some further negotiation but you end up with a $20,000 order for a single container. You send a pro forma invoice, the cash arrives in your bank and you ship the goods.

Four weeks later, you get another email. The goods reached Durban, they were cleared without difficulty and transported to the customer's warehouse in Port Elizabeth. The customer finds them even better than he hoped and expects to buy at least thirty containers over the next twelve months rising to eighty containers the following year. Eighty times $20,000 is $1.6 million. That's an additional two per cent on your turnover and you hardly had to do a thing to win it—the customer did all the work.

The customer did all the work. Ah, yes. As he now reminds you. He has opened this market for you and he feels exposed, because other people will see the sales he is making and they'll want to buy from you. Maybe they'll undercut him in the market. Is that fair reward for what he's done on your behalf? The way he got you into a market you hardly knew was there?

The customer wants exclusivity; a deal that says only he can buy your products for sale in Southern Africa. (Southern Africa? Doesn't he mean South Africa? But he explains that South Africa sets the lead for a bunch of neighbouring countries: Botswana, Lesotho, Mozambique, Namibia, Swaziland; and he can build your business there, too—as long as you protect him from unfair competition).

You kick it around in the office but, really, it's a no-brainer. You weren't doing business in South Africa—sorry, in Southern Africa—and now you are. And it's easy, because this guy down there does the work and all you have to do is bank the money and count the profits. A bit different from the cut-throat market in Europe. You write a letter, addressed To Whom It May Concern, saying that this man's company is your exclusive agent in Southern Africa and has the sole right to sell and distribute your products there. You get a company stamp made and stamp the letter because they do like their stamps in Africa (and in the Middle East, for that matter. And in Asia. You don't have a stamp? Get one made).

Would you appoint a salesperson to your own payroll without interviews? Psychometric tests? References? No? So what did you think you were doing, making this man you've never even met your sole representative over a huge chunk of territory?

Let's look at some of the things you don't know about him and his company. And when we've done that we'll think about the things you don't know about what you've given away.

How long has he been in business? What sort of business? How successfully? Has he ever been in trouble—with the law, the taxman, anyone? And his company—when was it formed? Who are its customers? What other suppliers does it have? Is it making money or losing it? What sort of reputation does it have in the market? And, since this is South Africa, where do this man and this company stand on the Black Empowerment Programme?

And that brings us nicely to the second thing I said we'd discuss: the things you don't know about what you've given away; because anyone wanting to do business in South Africa has to know about Black Empowerment. I go into that in more detail in Chapter 7, Continents and Countries—Specific Issues but there are other things about the territory that would have justified closer examination.

The customer's warehouse is in Port Elizabeth. Is that a good distribution centre for your goods? At this point, you probably don't know because you haven't done the research set out in Chapter 4. Port Elizabeth is a fair sized city with attractive beaches enjoyed by a population of three quarters of a million (and that probably excludes a lot of people there illegally) but it's right out on the Eastern Cape. South Africa is a big country and internal transport costs are a barrier to business. Something you needed to know before you gave anyone exclusive rights to sell there is either:

- Where do the kind of people who buy your goods live? *Or*

- Where are the kind of companies that buy your goods based?

Who is "your" man competing with? Is there a local manufacturer? Because, if there is, you need to know that the trend in South Africa is towards protecting local manufacturers by imposing tariff barriers (more on this in Chapter 7) and that $1.6 million could come under attack. Does the person you are dealing with have the political connections to resist protectionism?

And how realistic is that $1.6 million anyway? How big is the market for your products in South Africa? You don't know because you haven't done the research.

When someone makes the pitch for exclusivity this customer made (and they will make it, all the time—being a foreign manufacturer's exclusive agent is something many customers aim for and you will meet people who collect logos to show on their letterhead) the request can be handled easily enough. There's really only one sensible ground on which exclusivity should be granted and that is: performance. If someone says they can bring you $1.6 million p.a. in new business, and if you think $1.6 million would justify exclusive rights to a territory, then tell them they can be your exclusive agent but only after they have brought you sales of at least $1.6 million in a 12-month period. They won't be happy to leave it there—the argument will still be the same: how will you protect our interests in return for the market penetration we've given you?—and you could offer not to sell to anyone else in the territory for six months provided they achieve a level of sales in that time that shows they are making progress. In the case we are discussing, $1.6 million was the second year target—in the first twelve months they said they'd reach thirty containers or $600,000 but progress is rarely on a straight line so you might want to say that sales in those first six months should be not less than fifteen containers, or $300,000. There should be further targets and you may want to develop a new document—an Agreement to Agree. I've used such agreements successfully in cases like this.

If they refuse to accept this offer and hold out for immediate exclusivity, refuse. I have taken an increasingly hard line in this connection as decade has succeeded decade and I have never regretted saying No—though there have been times when I've wished we had not said Yes.

The example we've just worked through is merely one facet of something that will go on all the time if your products are in any way sought after. Make a sale in one place and someone from the city or country next door will contact you. If an Invitation to Tender is issued for which your products might be suitable, expect calls and emails from people you don't know. When you sell to ABC Ltd and they sell on to DEF Ltd, someone from DEF will contact you because they want to deal direct. In each case, you need to look closely at the kind of person or company they are and the kind of person or company you would get most value out of dealing with.

If you manufacture for the construction industry, contractors will be your end user—the people who buy the material in order to use it. Should you appoint a contractor as your agent? That should mean you get their business, but other contractors may not want to deal with a company they see as a competitor; so how dominant are they in their field? On the other hand, if you appoint a distributor who is not a contractor you have to be able to offer a price that allows the distributor to make a profit while still selling to contractors at a price they can pay. Maybe in this case you're better off selling to all contractors who want to buy from you, without a middle man at all—but if you do that you have to be prepared to go there regularly and stay long enough to see all your prospects.

When you make a splash—with a high profile sale; by getting Government approval for your products; after a successful exhibition—you will be inundated with approaches from people who want a share in your success. Whatever you do, take your time. If the opportunities are real, they won't go away.

## *Appointing a local representative*

If, after considering everything we've talked about so far, you decide you *do* need a local agent, you also need a lawyer. Tell a lawyer everything you can about your business and the deal you believe you have done with the agent-to-be and let the lawyer translate it into a binding legal contract. Some points, though:

- The contract has to say under what legal system it is to be interpreted and administered. Make sure it is your own. If you're in England and Wales, make it the legal system of England and Wales; in Scotland, the legal system of Scotland; in Germany, the German legal system; and so on. This won't usually be a problem but I have walked away from potentially good customers because I was not prepared to accept in one case, Saudi law, and in another, Libyan law and subsequent events did not cause me to regret it

- The agreement must include target levels of business— the amount of sales you expect to see. These should increase year-on-year and you should have the option to terminate the agreement if those levels are not reached

- The agreement should be for a fixed period. It can (and usually should) provide for automatic renewal and should make clear that renewal will not be unreasonably withheld, but it must be for a defined period

- A number of things should initiate immediate termination: bankruptcy or insolvency of either party; if either party is in breach or default of its obligations under this Agreement (it's usual to allow thirty days during which the offending party may remedy the breach); failure to achieve the minimum sales figures laid down; in the event of a change in ownership or management of the company having the agency, should that change be unacceptable to you; sale by the agent of products not manufactured by you which compete directly with yours

- Avoid territorial "add-ons". Your agent is in Kuwait and asks for exclusivity throughout the GCC (see Chapter 7 under Middle East), or is in Kenya and wants also to have Uganda, Tanzania and Democratic Republic of Congo. It sounds good, but do they have the salesforce and logistics in place to handle sales to those additional countries? Are they already selling there? Might it not be in your interest to find a second agent—one more suited to one or more of those additional countries?

- Watch out for lawyer creep. This is more likely to happen with large law firms than small ones and what I mean is that your lawyer wants to seek advice from another lawyer in the country where your agent operates. Resist this, because it will add a lot of cost and achieve nothing. If you're setting up a factory or a subsidiary company in another country then of course you need to make sure you're obeying the law there and you'd better have budgeted a lot of money for the purpose, but for a simple agency agreement you don't need it. You've already established that your agreement will operate under the law of your own country, so it will be in your country's courts that the agreement has to be enforced.

John Lynch

## *Supporting your local representative*

Supporting your local agent, distributor or customer is the single most important thing you have to do. You can't simply appoint an agent and then walk away and leave him to it. You will not get the sales you want that way.

One of the reasons you chose this company as your agent was that they have a big, well-managed salesforce. Nevertheless, they sell a lot of things and they can't possibly know your product as well as you do. They don't know the selling points that give it an edge over the competition; they don't know the questions to ask so that your product's advantages can be brought out; they haven't met the objections you've heard so often and they don't know how to handle a "no" so that it becomes a buying signal and then an order. You have to train them. That's part of your job.

How you do this will depend on the budget you have, because travel can become expensive, but I'm clear on the best method: you do it the way you would train your own salesforce. That is, in the classroom and on the road. If they have regular sales meetings, ask for a slot to present your product; if they don't, ask them to get their salespeople together (branch by branch works well) so that you can teach them what they need to know. Then go out on calls with individual salespeople. The first two or three times you do this, you should lead the call—if the salesperson is any good, s/he will pick up what you say, how you say it, the questions you ask, the way you answer questions and deal with objections. (If that does not happen, you face a task that no-one wants but that has to be accepted, which is to find a way to tell your agent that their salesperson is not up to the job. You will need all your tact to carry this off). After that, let the salesperson lead the call and discuss any problems afterwards. I find it essential to prepare a report after each call and send it to the salesperson and the salesperson's manager, setting out what happened and ending with a list of actions, naming the person who is to carry them out. Don't miss the opportunity (if it is justified) to congratulate the salesperson on a job well done, good customer relationship, clear product understanding—whatever.

Schedule your visits in the way that best meets your budget constraints and the agent's needs, but understand that there is an irreducible minimum; if you can't visit a country at least that minimum number of times, you have probably wasted the time and money spent on setting up the agency in the first place. I said in Chapter 2 that you have to go there and that compulsion does not reduce when you sign the agreement—if anything, it increases. Resist the temptation to think, "We've got someone on the ground now, so we can leave it to them". It doesn't work like that.

If the agent is doing her/his job (and if they aren't, what are you doing about it?) you will have a stream of emails and phone calls asking for your response to questions asked by the agent's customers. Can you answer this objection? Is the product suitable for that application? Should we reply to this invitation to tender? Reply as quickly as you can, and always in a way that will help the agent's workforce learn and be ready for the next similar question.

You will also hear from people who aren't your agent but have seen that your products are selling and want to get in on the act. If you have not granted exclusivity, fine, but if you have then you must reply copying your agent and say, "Our exclusive representative in [name country] is [your agent] and I am copying this email to them as I know they will wish to be in touch with you."

The word "catalogue" is one you will hear a lot because in some parts of the world it is expected that suppliers will have a catalogue and that they will make it available to anyone who asks. If you don't have a catalogue, you will probably find it worth producing one; loose leaf is best because these things can sit around on people's shelves for a very long time. Every time you produce a new insert is an excuse for you or one of your agent's staff to call on everyone who has a catalogue and update it—an excuse, because the thing salespeople find most difficult seems to be finding a new reason to call on a prospect.

When you have a new product, inform your customers and inform your agent. If the new introduction merits it, lay on training.

If you're selling to the construction industry, try to be there the first one or two times your product is installed. I have found these visits immensely valuable in heading off problems and misunderstandings before they arise.

# Chapter 7:
# Continents and Countries:
# Specific Issues

I could fill this book three times over with stuff about individual countries and regions, but that was not my purpose when I sat down to write an international sales handbook. What follow are some observations put together almost at random to say, "You may find these pointers helpful, but they're the tip of the iceberg. I hope they will whet your appetite and make you want to get out there into the wider world and start selling." If I tried to say everything there is to say about places like Saudi Arabia, South Africa and South Korea this book would become so long as to be unreadable. I'm not going to deal with every single country in the world, or even every country I've been to—I'll mention places about which I have something to say that might not be readily available on, say, Google.

## *Wrong Place, Wrong Time*

Let's start with the question of personal safety. Most places (not all—most) are safe most of the time. What you have to watch out for is Wrong Place, Wrong Time. It's killed or maimed a lot of people, and many of them were there to do business. I dealt with this in Chapter 2 under *Almost nowhere is as bad as the media say it is. But, just occasionally* ... so I won't repeat it here.

## *Africa*

The Dark Continent; the Heart of Darkness—a dangerous place. That's the general view of people who haven't been there. I usually say, 'Oh, Africa is no more dangerous than Moss Side in Manchester, or the rougher parts of Buffalo NY or Miami Fla.' Is that really true? No, it isn't. Parts of Africa are as dangerous as anywhere that isn't an actual war zone. Although Africa probably comes second to South America.

## Nigeria

Since I've already said some things about Nigeria, we'll start there. It isn't only physical danger you need to be concerned about, although you should accept that the north of the country is out of bounds to any visitor who is not a Salafist Moslem. Nigeria is the land of the scam and there is a very high level of dishonesty as well as corruption. You can do good business here, but you need to exercise caution. Oil has made the country rich but the money is not ploughed back into the economy. The banking system is efficient. The level of education is high. Private enterprise capitalism is encouraged, at least in the area south of the Niger and Benue rivers.

There is a (very rough) division of labour in that Army posts and many senior government jobs tend to be held by Moslems and private enterprise tends to be a Christian thing (I use the words tend and tends there—it isn't set in concrete). Don't let the fact that you're in a Christian company delude you. It's customary to begin meetings with a prayer for God's guidance, but starting a meeting with a prayer didn't prevent a company I visited from offering for sale, with our company's name on it, a product that was nothing to do with us.

I don't want to exaggerate this. I've dealt with some very sound and honest Nigerians—just don't assume that everyone is like that. You also need to know that they are extremely arrogant and quick to take offence even when no slight is intended.

## Ghana

I think of Ghanaians as the West Indians of Africa, by which I mean that they treat the world and everything in it as put there for their amusement. That doesn't stop them from working hard and they are (like the Nigerians next door) well educated and ambitious. You'll find Ghanaians in management positions all over West Africa, though they're not too keen on Nigeria. Good, reliable banking system. You can do good business here; it helps to know who you're going to see before you arrive (but that's true in most places).

## Other West African Countries

Nigeria and Ghana are where most people will find the bulk of their sales in West Africa. The Gambia, Sierra Leone and Senegal have also been good hunting grounds for me from time to time; I don't have enough experience of the others to make meaningful comments and I put that down to the fact that they don't have any money—if there's one obvious rule it is: go where the money is. By and large, countries like Burkina Faso and Niger will only be customers worth the expense of courtship when an international funding body is putting up the money.

## South Africa

Where to start on the Republic of South Africa? It's big and it's varied—in languages, in ethnic origins of its people, in height above sea level, in appearance...I could go on. I've done good business there and so have many other people; it can't be ignored. There's a good banking system, good education and a growing black middle class; at the same time there is widespread poverty (from which the less well-educated whites are not immune). The word "black", by the way, is often avoided in favour of "previously disadvantaged". It's sometimes a dangerous country and visitors from Europe can be surprised to learn just how many people are carrying concealed handguns.

Choose your customer or your agent carefully. I know this will antagonise a number of South Africans for whom I have great respect, but I recommend you choose someone who is previously disadvantaged—to put it plainly, not white. If you choose a large company it will probably be white in origin and, mainly, in management because sought-after redistribution of control has not yet been seen, but check its BEE credentials.

BEE stands for Black Economic Empowerment. The theory of immediate post-Apartheid times that getting blacks into senior positions in government and industry would trickle down to improve the position of blacks everywhere has not worked. Any attempt to sum up the current position on BEE will be out of date very quickly because the Government is becoming firmer and the situation changes quite quickly, but the South African Government has a useful website that should tell you the latest position: http://tinyurl.com/m5v224g. You should talk to a South African lawyer, but don't try to do it by getting a lawyer in your own country to ask the questions. Go There. You won't get the correct picture unless you talk to people on the ground. But be aware that the Government of South Africa is increasingly prepared to use compulsion to get the results it wants.

Be aware also that the South African government adopts protectionist policies. As I write this, the Rand (the South African currency) is doing better than it has done recently but plot its history on a graph and the trend is down. When the Rand was first introduced in 1961 it was at the rate of two to the British Pound. Today it is worth just over one tenth of that. Faced with that kind of slide, the Government places great value on replacing imports with locally manufactured goods.

Something else you need to beware of in South Africa is double invoicing. (This also applies in a number of other African countries). Countries that are short of foreign exchange impose exchange control, restricting the free movement of money out of the country. Britain had exchange controls for forty years from 1939 and many countries have them today, including some (like Nigeria, Russia and India) that you might think of as well off. (Exchange control isn't always about being hard up—it can be introduced to prevent money laundering (it doesn't work) or simply to tighten government control over every aspect of its citizen's lives). Every salesperson who deals with a country that has exchange control will be asked from time to time to provide two invoices—the "real" one and an inflated one that the customer will use to get central bank approval to transfer out of the country more money than is required by the import. If you agree, you will be breaking the law of the country with which you are doing business—so don't. I know just how much sympathy it's possible to feel with the customer who needs to send money to his aged parents in Holland or to finance his daughter's education in Germany, and I know that refusing can cost you the customer's business—it makes no difference. I've heard people say that preventing people from sending money they have earned to any place they choose is wrong—I don't care. I've lost customers in South Africa, Zimbabwe and elsewhere by refusing to double invoice and I'd do it again. Do you really want to risk not being able to go back to a country because you're on their wanted list? Or, worse, to face an extradition hearing?

## Other Southern African countries

South Africa casts a long and largely benevolent shadow and countries around its borders (and inside, in the case of Botswana) take their lead from the Saffers in many things. Mozambique has a strong Portuguese influence and is well worth visiting in its own right even though it is a very poor country, but Botswana, Namibia, Lesotho and Swaziland are all part of the Southern African Customs Union (SACU) and you should approach them as part of your South African campaign. Distinguish between this and the larger Southern African Development Community (SADC) some of which—especially Mozambique, Angola (another country with a Portuguese history), Tanzania, Malawi, Zambia and Zimbabwe—are best targeted directly.

## East Africa

Although Tanzania is part of the SADC it is also, along with Kenya, Tanzania, Uganda, Rwanda and Burundi, a member of the East African Community. When I began selling there a long time ago, the first three of these countries (actually, Tanzania was at that time Tanganyika and had not absorbed Zanzibar) were a tight East African grouping sharing a common currency, the East African Shilling. They are a graphic illustration that countries with different ideas on taxation and political theory should not share a currency. The East African Community planned to reintroduce a common currency in 2012; it slipped and is now proposed for 2015. Personally, I can't see it happening.

If you were only going to sell in one East African country, it should be Kenya which is easily the most prosperous. Pick the right Kenyan partner and you will find that they also have salespeople in Uganda, Rwanda and Burundi.

Kenya can be dangerous, especially if you get close to the border with Somalia (which I suggest you don't). Nairobi is the capital and Mombasa is the port. Mombasa is hot and uncomfortably humid; Nairobi is high above sea level and pleasant. People will tell you that walking around Nairobi on your own is an invitation to muggers but I've strolled around there at night with a laptop in my hand and never had any trouble.

When Daniel Arap Moi was President (1978 to 2002) what happened to Kenya's foreign currency earnings is still shrouded in mystery and infrastructure was neglected. The railway from Mombasa to Uganda by way of Nairobi is still in poor condition and Nairobi Airport is frankly awful. The roads aren't much better and getting around Nairobi can be desperately slow. The present Government is trying hard to improve matters. I recommend staying out of Kenya during elections; it's a tribal country and riots are frequent and bloody. It usually calms down quickly afterwards. Education is good and there is a growing middle class, but the majority of Kenya's population still lives in desperate poverty.

Over the past ten years I've done eight times as much business in Kenya as in the other four countries added together. Nevertheless, Tanzania can be a good market if you have the right products for them—but they're big customers of China and price will be a more important factor than quality.

## North Africa

Egypt and Libya are often grouped with the Middle East, and I can see the sense of that, but geographically they're in Africa. Those two countries, together with Tunisia, are where what people call the Arab Spring started, and putting them in this section gives me the chance to say:

- It wasn't a spring as I understand the word; *and*

- It was, in any case, a Mediterranean phenomenon.

In keeping with my advice not to get involved with other people's politics, I'll say no more about the first of those points; concerning the second, I'll have something to say about the use of the word "Arab" when I get to the Middle East.

This southern fringe of the Mediterranean has a fascinating history. In the West we're familiar with the word "Moor" (Othello was a Moor) and Moors were originally the inhabitants of what is now known as the Maghreb (currently Morocco, Algeria, Tunisia together with, unaccountably, Mauritania). The Maghreb was also known as Barbary which comes from the Berber people who are still numerous. The Romans were here, the Phoenicians were here, the Byzantines were here, the Ottoman Empire was here. Why am I telling you this in a book about selling? Because the favourite occupation of Berbers, Phoenicians and Turks in this area was piracy and I suggest you bear that in mind when you are doing business there. The people are, by and large, polite but they are proud and they expect fair dealing; if they think they're not getting it, they will respond accordingly.

Libya has oil and, therefore, money—though it is not as rich as many people (including its own) think it is and it will be stretched if it attempts to do all of the repair, maintenance and development work that needs to be done. I've done good business here over the years and you can, too. I've also done good business in Egypt, and Egypt is not a rich country; in fact, it's poor. I've had less success in Tunisia and almost none in Morocco and Algeria; if you want to sell there, you'll do best with a salesperson whose native language is French.

Something you need to be aware of in Libya is that everyone is aware of how much corruption there was in the Gaddafi days. If you wanted to sell then, you needed an agent who was (the term most widely used) "family". S/he didn't have to be a Gaddafi relative but did need good connections with someone who was. Today, when Libya still has an interim Government, officials are afraid of being charged with corruption even when completely innocent. For example, the decision to build a new road will be met with: "Why do you want to build it there? Does your family own property that will benefit?" For this reason, studies are very popular; if the minister in question can produce an independent survey that says this is the best route for a proposed road, the corruption question can be dealt with. It follows that almost all decisions take a long time and you need to stay on top of the matter—keep in contact, go there if you can, get to know all the people involved.

Libya has three provinces: Tripolitania; Cyrenaica; and Fezzan. Tripolitania is the northwest, capital Tripoli (also the capital of Libya itself); Cyrenaica (capital Benghazi) is the northeast, butting up against the border with Egypt; and the Fezzan is the (largely desert) area to the southwest. The people of the Fezzan probably have as much in common with the populations of Niger and Chad as with the rest of Libya. I asked British consular officials in Tripoli whether they believed Libya would continue to exist as one country and they said it would, with a sufficient degree of federalism granting powers to the provinces. They may believe this or it may be British government policy to say so; either way, I am not convinced.

If you go to Tripoli, go to Misrata as well—it's a thriving place and there's a lot of business to be done there. But when you go to Libya, you will need kidnap and ransom insurance and it's a good idea to work with one of the security companies (like Salamanca Risk Management, who I mentioned in Chapter 4) to stay as safe as possible.

**NOTE** I wrote the section immediately above (on Libya) in May 2014. In July, things changed. I've made clear my reservations about media reports, but I stayed in close touch with my contacts on the ground and as a result of what they told me I wrote this report for my boss:

Libya has had its election and now has a government with something resembling legitimacy—but no power. IS (or ISIS), the terrorist group looking to set up a "Caliphate" in Syria and Iraq, has been establishing itself in and around Benghazi (because that is where the readiest access to oil and, therefore, money is) and the government has turned a blind eye— probably because it had no power to do anything about it. The official line has been that these are not terrorists and their intentions have been good and it is true that IS has followed the line previously taken by the Moslem Brotherhood in Egypt who worked out that the best way to get people on their side was to be seen as helping ordinary people get what they needed. Soldiers and policemen were being assassinated regularly in Benghazi but IS said they were not responsible and the government chose not to dispute this, at least in public. Someone was bound to intervene and the someone was General Khalifa Hifter who had been a general in Gadaffi's forces and defected to the Libyan rebel army in 2011. General Hifter set up what amounts to his own army to combat all of the militias threatening peace in Libya with particular emphasis on IS. As xxx put it, (I have deleted this name to protect a source) "If he succeeds, the government loses because he is not part of the government. If he fails, the government loses anyway." The feeling among ordinary Libyans is that he won't fail, but success won't come quickly.

One good result of Hifter's intervention is that IS declared themselves and there is now no doubt that they were responsible for deaths of soldiers and policemen and (at least some of) the occasional carjacking and murder of civilians. There have been pitched battles and the risks a visit would involve are now too great to ignore.

So, yes, it's tough in Libya right now—but the opportunities are still there. I believe that calm will be restored and that Libya will once again be a good place to do business. If you're going to do business in places like this, you need that sort of network; if you don't have one, find someone you can trust who does.

Egypt is a great place to do business provided you have what they want. It's possible to be misled by what you read. In their first free elections they voted in a Moslem Brotherhood Government and were portrayed as Islamic extremists who wanted to drive Israel into the sea, but this is nonsense. The majority of the population is secular by inclination. They voted for the Brotherhood because under the Mubarak regime, when they had needed a home, medical care or a school for their children, it was the Brotherhood that had helped them—the liberals had wrung their hands and said how awful everything was but offered no practical help. When the Egyptian people saw that the aim of the Morsi Government was to make sure that their first free election was also their last, they wanted to get rid of it. Whatever you may read, the majority of the population is in favour of the military intervention that took place in 2013.

If you are selling to the construction industry, you may find it helpful to know that Cairo University turns out some of the best civil engineers in the world—and half of them are women. That's another reason why Egyptians are happy with the military's removal of Morsi—women in Egypt are valued as men's equals and they could see that equality going down the pan if Morsi continued in power (a fear shared by Turkish women under their present government). Do not, though, get into an argument with a male Egyptian engineer. Even if you are 100% right, you won't win. He can't let you.

## *The Middle East*

There's a huge amount of money in the Middle East, and places with lots of money are an obvious sales target, but not all countries there are rich. The ones with money to spend are: Saudi Arabia, Qatar, Oman, Bahrain, Kuwait and the UAE (United Arab Emirates). I'll also include Turkey in that list, though there must be disagreement over whether Turkey is geographically in the Middle East as opposed to Europe or Asia. Jordan and Yemen are poor relations, while Syria and Iraq have problems of their own and Iran is currently embargoed (though I'm hopeful that Western governments will eventually see how nonsensical that is).

The word "Arab" is misused, or at least misunderstood. Increasingly today, "Arab" is used to mean "opponent of Israel," which is odd when we remember that Arabs can be Moslem, Jewish, Christian or even something else entirely. Countries are thought of as Arabic when Arabic is the main language, which would make Iraqis, Egyptians and Syrians Arabs; if you want a peaceful life, I suggest you don't use the word to their faces. Personally, I only use it to describe someone from the Arabian peninsula and their descendants. So, for me, an Arab would be a person of any religion from Saudi Arabia, the UAE, Kuwait, Oman, Yemen, Bahrain or Qatar; I'm aware that many people would disagree.

Another point of nomenclature to beware of is variations on "The Gulf". I grew up referring to The Persian Gulf and that seemed to be standard at that time, but now you will hear three versions:

- The Persian Gulf;

- The Iranian Gulf; *and*

- The Arabian Gulf.

It may seem that this is a small thing and that it doesn't matter which expression you use, but it really does. Iranians say, "It's ours" and they are annoyed by "Arabian Gulf" to the point that they will refuse to deal with anyone who uses that expression. Inhabitants of the GCC (Gulf Co-operation Council) states feel the same way about "Persian Gulf" or "Iranian Gulf"; their more temperate mindset means that they will merely think you ignorant or discourteous and not shout at you (or worse) as an Iranian might—but what salesperson looking for an order wants to be thought ignorant or discourteous by a prospect? Adjust the term you use to the person you're talking to.

If you're going to try doing business in the Middle East, one of the first things to go into your diary every year should be the start and end dates of the holy month of Ramadan. Because the Moslem calendar follows a lunar year instead of the 365 day model, Ramadan moves forward a little each Western year. It is a time for fasting, meditation and prayer. During Ramadan, Moslems are required to refrain from eating, drinking (including water), smoking and sex during the hours of daylight. Although people work, imagine how much concentration you would be capable of during the later daylight hours when you had not been allowed to eat or drink anything and, if you are a smoker, to smoke. Do not think of Ramadan as being like Lent, which in most of Christendom has been reduced to giving up a little something—Ramadan is taken seriously and you must take it seriously, too. Do not be seen in public eating, drinking so much as a glass of water or smoking. This is not a small matter; you will not be forgiven. In places like the UAE your behaviour will be treated as discourteous; in Saudi Arabia it will be an offence that may be punished. When you go to someone else's country, respect their ways.

## Saudi Arabia

I start here because Saudi Arabia is the biggest (with Turkey) and the richest. The money comes from oil, of which it has huge amounts. Saudi Arabia is one of the six GCC (Gulf Co-operation Council) countries.

# The International Sales Handbook

A lot of people will tell you they don't like going to Saudi. I do. Of course, I'm a man—women do go there on business and they sometimes succeed but personally I would not ask a woman to cover Saudi because the conditions under which she would have to work would be onerous. Fly in, go to one meeting, fly out—fine. But spend a week there visiting three customers each day? Very difficult.

You have to accept (as you always must) that you're in someone else's country and their laws, customs and expectations are to be respected. The legal system is Sharia law; the Koran and the Sunnah are the constitution. Alcohol and drugs are not permitted and the penalties are severe. Homosexual acts and adultery are against the law and can be (and are) punished by beheading. Women are not allowed to drive and must be covered in public. Restaurants have "family sections;" if you're a man on his own, or in a group of men, stay out of them because they are for women—women on their own; women with men to whom they are related by marriage or by blood; women with children. It is an offence for a man and woman to be together in public (it's an even greater offence in private) unless they are married or close blood relations. (And married means married—the fact that you've lived with each other for twenty years won't alter the fact that you're breaking Saudi law by being in each other's company). Women are employed in business, contrary to what many people think, but they will have their own room and a man who wants to speak to them must knock on the door to give them time to cover up and wait until instructed to enter. As well as the police, the Committee for the Promotion of Virtue and the Prevention of Vice, also known as Haia or Mutaween ("the pious") and generally referred to as the Religious Police, may carry out spot checks. The only religion allowed to be practised is Islam; churches are not permitted and neither are private prayer meetings. Proselytising, or even expressing a view of Islam that might in any way be considered negative, is a terrorist act and punished accordingly. If you're not Moslem then parts of Mdina and all of Macca (or Mecca) are out of bounds; break that rule and you can get not just yourself but the people who took you there stoned to death.

The climate can be difficult—temperatures in summer can exceed 50ºC (122ºF).

And still I like it. Why? Well, all I've given you so far is what you may think of as negatives. There's plenty on the other side of the ledger.

When the Prophet Mohamed was asked "What is religion?" he replied that religion is akhlaq, and that akhlaq is good conduct and morality. Not to be angry is akhlaq. Akhlaq means showing good manners and courtesy. And that is what the people do. (You will find the same attitude in the UAE, in Kuwait, in Oman and elsewhere in the Arab world).

Jeddah is on the Red Sea and the seafood is wonderful. (Jeddah is also by far the most liberal city in Saudi Arabia; Riyadh, Dammam and Khobar probably the least so). It is, by and large, a peaceful country where you can feel at ease walking anywhere, even late at night. It almost never rains. Temperatures during the winter months are very pleasant.

Arabs are not good at conflict and, because they are not good at it, they don't like it—it makes them uncomfortable. Because they don't like it, avoiding it is a good idea. When you have something that has to be discussed, find a non-confrontational way to do it. Whatever you do, don't lose your temper.

As in all Moslem countries, prayer time happens five times a day. Unlike most other Moslem countries, it's enforced here—everything has to stop. Restaurants lock their doors. Kiosks close. People leave their desks and counters to pray. You will find prayer places all over office and factory buildings. You can tell that's what they are from the rug on the floor. Whatever you do, do not walk on the rug with your shoes on. In fact, if you're not Moslem you'd do best to stay off it entirely.

One more thing before we leave Saudi Arabia. If you don't like what I've said about it; if it offends you; if you think, "I'm a free-born American/cantankerous Englishman/ enlightened Scot/all-conquering German/condescending Frenchman and

I'm not going to be told what to do"—stay away from the Middle East in general and Saudi Arabia in particular. If you decide that no-one's going to tell you what you can and can't say and, anyway, we're all the same underneath, aren't we, and you just know that these people really want what you want which is good healthy discussion—find somewhere else to sell. If you don't know how to keep your mouth shut, stay home.

## The United Arab Emirates (UAE)

A GCC country. There are seven Emirates in the United Arab Emirates: Abu Dhabi (the capital), Dubai, Sharjah, Fujairah, Ras al Khaimah, Ajman and Umm al-Quwain. The most important from a business point of view are: Abu Dhabi, Dubai and Sharjah. Anyone who has been to Dubai on holiday will feel that it is very different from Saudi Arabia as I have described it and it is true that the UAE is more liberal than Saudi—but it's still a Moslem country and you still need to behave.

Alcohol is permitted in hotel bars and some restaurants, though not in hotel lobbies. Women are not required to be covered, though some choose to be. The standard of education is good and visitors are well received, BUT everyone wants to do business here and the competition is fierce. This is also a place where, if you're not careful, the lowest quality can set the price—they want something better but they don't want to pay more than the cheapest product on the market would cost.

For construction materials, the UAE is the land of the sample. You can cover the place (and some people do) with free demonstrations of your product without ever getting an order. Two lessons most people selling construction materials in the UAE eventually learn are:

- People don't value what they haven't paid for; *and*

- Asking for a sample is often a polite way to get rid of the visitor.

If you agree to carry out a sample for which you are not being paid:

- Make sure you find out how the sample will be monitored and judged;

- Confirm your understanding in writing; *and*

- Follow up to make sure that what you agreed is being done.

## Jordan

Not a GCC country. Jordan does not have a lot of money and it does have a lot of problems. They buy things, however. Companies shipping American goods have an edge because Jordan enjoys most favoured nation status with the USA and the rate of import duty on goods from America is low.

## Lebanon

Not a GCC country. Beirut is a beautiful city and safe to visit. Other parts of the country are less so. Westerners should stay well away from the borders with Israel and Syria. The population is only four million but imports in 2012 amounted to US$21.3 billion, so there's business to be done there. There's a lot of corruption and getting things through Customs without making a small payment to an official can be hit and miss. The Lebanese are traders by nature and can make good agents and representatives (and not only in Lebanon) but you need to choose carefully and you need to keep a close eye on what is happening. Your Lebanese customer will think nothing of buying your (good) product and adulterating it with something cheap. When one man there told me that that was what another customer was doing I said, "Of course you'd never do such a thing." He slapped me on the back and laughed. Life in Lebanon can be precarious and no-one should be surprised when someone living from day to day helps himself to what, really, belongs to someone else.

Beirut is also a good place to meet customers from Iraq or

Syria when conditions make a visit there too risky to contemplate. Don't leave without visiting a seafood restaurant at least once.

## Oman

A GCC country. Oman is prosperous and safe, though extra precautions are sensible if you're going near the border with Yemen. It is a country where, ideally, you need a local representative and I recommend great care in choosing who that agent should be—Oman has more than its share of logo collectors. Documents have to be legalised and, in theory, products require labelling in Arabic but unless your goods are to be sold in the retail trade you can assume that this is not so.

## Kuwait

A GCC Country. Kuwait is small but has productive oilfields and is therefore rich.

## Syria

Damascus has for many years been my favourite city anywhere in the world. I hate to see what's happening to it now and I don't know whether I'll ever get back there. If you'd asked me four years ago I'd have said that Damascus was safe to walk around in the middle of the night and you might want to bear that in mind when you read my other observations on safety—things can change. Syria is completely corrupt; don't try to do business there without understanding that.

## Iraq

*I wrote this section before the troubles of July 2014 broke out and I believe that what I say has been vindicated.* I'm sorry, Mr Obama, Mr Hague, Ms Ashton, I don't care what you say—Iraq is not one country and cannot survive as one.

If you're looking to sell there, mount two campaigns—one in the south and one in Iraqi Kurdistan (which may soon be simply Kurdistan) in the north. If you sell to Kurdistan, don't try to ship through the Iraqi port, Umm Qasr—the Iraqis will often prevent goods landed there from reaching the people in the north who actually paid for them. Instead, ship to the Turkish port, Mersin—the Kurds will clear them and ship to Erbil or anywhere else in the north. Either way, you need pre-inspection by SGS or Bureau Veritas.

You can get a visa on arrival in Kurdistan but for the rest of Iraq you need a visa before you go and to get it you must show that you have kidnap and ransom insurance. A side effect of this is that some of the people who watch you get off the plane aren't actually looking at a human being—what they see is a walking ATM.

## Iran

I thought long and hard before saying this, but in the end I decided I should. Iranians are among the most charming people in the world—courteous, educated, outgoing, civilised—but I don't believe I've ever met a completely sane one. There. I've said it.

I hope to see the embargoes lifted soon and I hope to do business with Iran before I retire but I'm cautious about going there. Their Government thinks nothing of arresting westerners for offences they know they have not committed and holding them for prolonged periods as bargaining tools in disputes with other countries. Charming, educated and civilised or not, the Enlightenment never happened in Iran. The individual counts for nothing; only the State matters.

Don't, though, take everything at face value. There can be fierce demonstrations against the West but they're put on by the government and not always meant by the people taking part. One morning in Teheran I asked the hotel's concierge to call a taxi to take me to my prospect's office. 'There would be no point, sir. There is a demonstration. A car could not get through.' I asked what the demonstration was about but he was reluctant to tell me. When I stepped outside the hotel, which the concierge clearly did not want me to do, I could hear chanting from somewhere not far away. I walked to the end of the street. The chanting was louder now and I could see that the crowds probably were too big to force a way through without inflaming tempers. I was glad I did not have a flight to catch. There was a pavement café nearby and I decided to have a coffee and a pastry (Teheran has attractive cafés with good coffee and nice pastries). The waiter was more forthcoming than the concierge; when I asked what the demonstrators were chanting he said, "Kill the Americans. Kill the British." Oh. Right. Okay. I sipped my coffee. As always happens, a man idling his time away stopped by my table and asked where I was from. 'The UK.' He pulled out a chair, sat down at my table and called to some other men standing in the road listening to the mob. 'This guy's from England.' (The idea that Britain, the UK and England are not all words describing the same area of land seems impossible for the non-British to grasp. Wales? Scotland? Northern Ireland? That's England, isn't it?) I soon had half a dozen people at my table (once again as always happens). Something Teheran has in common with Damascus is that, if four or more men are sitting at a table, at least one of them will be an informer if not a full time secret policeman. I didn't have to remind myself of that because it isn't something I ever forget. The conversation followed its usual course: this man had a sister living in Milton Keynes—did I know her? That one had been accepted by a college in Sunderland but then came the revolution and he hadn't been able...did I understand? I did. And then came the one question you always know you're going to get. "If I give you my CV, can you get me a job in your country?"

And all the time, the mob was chanting that I and all my compatriots should be hanging from a tree. When you meet with apparent hostility, don't assume it's serious.

## *North America*

Not much to say here—if you're reading this in the States or Canada you already know everything there is to know and if you're anywhere else just turn on your TV or go to the cinema.

Don't call Canadians American. They don't react as actively as Scots who you've called English, but they don't like it. And be aware of the Not Invented Here antipathy that has buried many good foreign ideas in America.

Keep in mind how big these countries are. A Canadian once told me a Canadian joke (yes, I know, but apparently they do have them). A family in Britain write to their friends in Vancouver: "The Smiths have emigrated to Nova Scotia. Why don't you drop in and see them?" Back comes the reply: "Why don't you? You're nearer." And it's true—the east coast of Canada is nearer to Europe than it is to the west coast of Canada.

Two other things for Europeans selling in North America to remember:

- Odd it may be, but they are often more formal in dress and manners than European businessmen; *and*

- They don't drink anything like as much alcohol as many Europeans.

## South America

I talked about danger in Africa and parts of the Middle East. It's easy to overlook the dangers in South America. Colombia, Venezuela, Brazil and Mexico are as dangerous as anywhere in the world and Argentina, El Salvador and Honduras aren't far behind.

It's useful to be a Spanish or Portuguese speaker in much of South America.

For the most part, education levels are not high. In most countries there is a small, educated elite and a huge, less well-educated mass.

I've given up apologising for my negative approach to South America. It's thirty years since I was first told that Brazil was on the verge of shaking the world with its advance—the place to invest; the place you had to be. I'm still waiting.

## Chile

It's pronounced "cheelay" and not "chilly" and it's the most prosperous country in South America and the best one to do business in. It's only the fifth largest economy on the continent but it has the highest GDP and it achieved that by putting more stress on education than the others and allowing greater freedom; the middle class is bigger here than elsewhere in South America and growing. Low tariff barriers are a help. You really do need to speak Spanish, however.

## Argentina

Argentina should come second after Chile as a place to do business with, but the economy is in a far worse state than they want you to know, inflation is rampant, the country is as bad as Iceland at meeting its debts and Argentine politicians are even more dishonest than the global norm (which isn't good). On the plus side, education is widespread and many people speak English though they can suddenly forget how when it suits them—once again, you really need to speak Spanish. And when you've shaken hands— count your fingers. (All still there? Good.)

## Columbia

I have a soft spot for Columbia and I really like the people. They're educated, outgoing and friendly. It's very dangerous, though.

## *Europe*

This section is written primarily for readers who are not themselves European. I'm British—in fact, English (yes, there is a difference, which I will spell out). I was for a couple of years salesman for French-speaking and German-speaking Europe which was somehow extended to include places like Holland, Denmark and Scandinavia and for several years as International Sales Director in three different companies I managed salespeople selling across the globe including the whole of Europe but most of my sales career has been outside

Europe (long haul, if you like). What I'm going to say here is what I hope will be some useful generalisations.

Europe is not a country. There are politicians, both elected and unelected, who would like a huge chunk of Europe to become a federation of states on the American model but for now and the foreseeable future Europe is a continent inhabited by about fifty separate countries depending on how you decide who is in Europe and who is not. It's the second smallest continent in land area but the third largest in population—only Asia and Africa have more people. You can split Europe in several different ways: East and West; North and South; rich and poor; Eurozone and non-Eurozone; EU and non-EU and how you define where the borders of Europe are can say as much about you as it does about the place itself. Personally, I would count Russia, Turkey and Cyprus as in Europe and I would also include Israel but the reason for the last named is that you cannot have salespeople who sell to Saudi Arabia, Libya, Syria and a number of other Middle Eastern countries also calling on Israel. Is Kazakhstan in Europe? It is to me.

## Great Britain and the United Kingdom

Britain is not called Great out of vainglory; it's a name given to it at least as early as 150AD to distinguish it from Little Britain, or Ireland. There are three countries in Great Britain: England, Scotland and Wales. It is a common mistake to call the Welsh and the Scots English and one I suggest you don't make if you're looking to sell in either Scotland or Wales. Also try to remember that Scots are Scottish, not Scotch—that name is reserved for whisky. Something else to bear in mind if this is where you see one of your markets: I've had great success in employing Scottish salespeople to cover northern England but it doesn't work the other way round. I don't doubt that Americans, Kazakhs, South Africans and Martians would be cordially received but Scottish tolerance does not extend to the English.

Northern Ireland is not part of Great Britain but when you add it to the mix you get the United Kingdom of Great Britain and Northern Ireland, normally shortened to "the UK". Scotland may decide to leave the UK, in which case I'll rewrite this section.

The UK is in the European Union (EU), for the moment at least, but is not part of the Eurozone; the currency is the Pound.

## Germany

The motor of the EU and the Eurozone. Doing business in Germany is always a pleasure.

## Holland

It's really The Netherlands but Holland will do. A good place to do business and has the largest ports in Europe. Eurozone.

## France

Eurozone. Has lived in the economic shadow of Germany for some years. Manages to protect its industries while operating in an EU that forbids protectionism. Make sure you understand exactly what it is you've agreed and that you have it written down.

## Ireland

Eurozone. Has been through a bad time economically over the past few years and has a small population but there's business to be done there.

## Spain, Portugal and Italy

With the occasional addition of Greece, this is what is usually meant by "Southern Europe" and there's a lot more going on there than many people think. Well worth a visit.

Eurozone. There's corruption in all these countries with star billing going to Italy. There must—surely—be at least one Italian government employee who isn't bent—if you find him or her, let me know because I certainly haven't.

## Greece

Eurozone. Basket case. If you sell here, get the money up front or insist on a Letter of Credit and make sure it's confirmed by a solid bank in your own country.

## Cyprus

Eurozone. Paid a heavy penalty for an economy that supported dead weight and refused to face reality. They'll climb out of it.

## *Scandinavia and the Nordic Countries*

I phrase it that way to avoid a tedious correspondence on which countries really constitute Scandinavia. I include in that term Norway, Denmark, Sweden, Iceland and Finland; others will tell you that only the first three are in Scandinavia while Iceland and Finland join them to make up the Nordic Countries.

Denmark, Sweden and Finland are in the EU; Norway and Iceland are not. Only Finland is in the Eurozone.

When I talked about North Africa I reminded readers that the people were once pirates; dealing with Scandinavia it is as well not to put completely out of your mind that this is where the Vikings came from. Scandinavians can seem peaceful, civilised, friendly people—and for the most part they are—but they will always punch above their weight and they can be counted on to defend their position. They are convinced by facts, not marketing ploys.

They like good, clean design (I'm writing this with a Skagen watch on my wrist and I wouldn't swap it for a Rolex or anything else). They also value reliability and honesty. Nokia is a high tech company known around the world and its history tells us a lot about Scandinavians. Nokia began as a logging and milling company—there are an awful lot of trees in Finland—selling wood products. That is a very cyclical business to be in and they went into mobile phones to have a more secure future and to exploit the very high standard of education in Finland. From there (and this is where I became involved) they went into IT peripheral equipment manufacture and, soon, bought Ericsson's 3270 subsidiary. This had once been a good product for the Swedish company Ericsson but it had been allowed to stagnate and was losing market share. (3270 is a means of communication with IBM mainframes and Ericsson had made the decision—which proved to be wrong—to stay with a system-compatible instead of a plug-compatible approach). Nokia changed the approach and developed a range of equipment that rapidly regained market share (of course, brilliant salesmanship did no harm ☺) and eventually sold out to Fujitsu.

Working like that with people from the Nordic countries taught me a few things that may be useful. Chief among those is that this is not a monolithic bloc of five like-minded countries—there is a rivalry and sometimes an antipathy between them. The Swedes had difficulty accepting that the Finns—a bunch of farmers and bumpkins as far as they were concerned—could do a better high tech job than them. Danes, Norwegians and Finns, all of whom had a bad time during WWII, resented the way the Swedes had preserved their neutrality by cutting runways out of their forests for the convenience of Luftwaffe aircraft. You'll now be dealing with the grandchildren of the people of that time, but don't assume that the ill will has gone away.

Nevertheless, these are generally good countries for outsiders to do business with and in; the exception is Iceland. The difficulties caused when Iceland refused to repay foreigners who had lost money in their bank collapse has been well publicised but did not come out of the blue. I'm not going to say that Icelanders are untrustworthy but I am going to say—and this is the result of twenty years experience and not simply the bank collapse—that you should: examine very carefully the terms you agree; make sure that both parties know what they are and that they are in writing; take careful credit checks before granting credit and renew them annually; and try to have transactions underwritten by a bank either through a Letter of Credit or by Cash Against Documents.

A last word about the Finns—they work by committee and by consensus. They won't make a decision until everyone has bought in—but then they'll want execution immediately. This approach (which the Japanese also follow) means there's no-one in the company with that "This won't work because I won't let it" attitude one meets in Britain and elsewhere, but it also means that sometimes you have to wait for a decision.

## Eastern Europe

I've done business in Poland, Hungary and the Czech Republic but I'd be misleading you if I claimed enough knowledge to guide your operations there.

## Turkey

I've heard people say that Turks are untrustworthy and that you can't enforce judgements against them. That has not been my experience. Provided that you choose your partner carefully, Turkey can be an excellent place to do business. Things to pay close attention to:

- Make sure the company or person is financially stable

- Look at the credit records carefully—are bills paid on time?

- Have there been any legal problems?

There is a high level of education in the cities. The language is Turkish but English and Arabic are widely spoken. Links with Iraqi Kurdistan are good—amazingly so given the number of Kurds killed by Turkey over the years. Since the days of Kemal Ataturk, Turkey has been a secular country (like Egypt) but in the last few years there has been a determined attempt (as in Egypt) to transform it into an Islamic state and (unlike Egypt) this attempt has so far been successful. None of that should prevent anyone from doing business there.

## *Australia and New Zealand*

The language is English, the level of education is high, they're open to new ideas and ways of operating—and, if you're in Europe or North America, they're a long way away so you need to plan your visits carefully to get the maximum return on your money.

People generally split between those who like Australia and those who prefer New Zealand. Personally, I'm a NZ man. I should think most people have heard the old joke about the airline pilot who says, "Ladies and gentlemen, welcome to Auckland International Airport. Please set your watches back fifty years." I like that about Kiwis—the fact that they retain the courtesy and politeness you once found in Britain but no longer do. They are good to do business with, appreciate quality and are prepared to pay for it—but most are only two generations at most away from farming stock and they retain that farmer's wish (and ability) to make do and mend and get the maximum life out of a product.

The Australian economy has done well in recent years and there are opportunities there.

Don't go to either of these countries expecting to be in and out in a day or two. I generally planned my Anzac trips to be three weeks long and it paid off. Line up your visits well in advance, rent a car (and a satnav) and cover as much ground as you can.

## *South East Asia*

It's a huge area; the countries I've done business with are: China, India, Malaysia, Indonesia, South Korea and Japan and that's what I will concentrate on.

I've heard many times that the people in these countries are not to be trusted and it simply isn't so. I find the people in Japan honest.

When I talked about Lebanon I said that you could not be surprised if people who lived in countries where life and success were precarious put their own interests in front of yours. If things go wrong, they have no safety net. Something I learned early in dealing with China, Indonesia and Malaysia is to make sure agreements were in writing and that they covered absolutely everything. People there are likely to assume that anything not explicitly excluded is okay. Example:

A company based in Europe set up a South East Asian subsidiary and hired a manager to run it. They did not understand why the subsidiary did not make as much profit as they had expected. When they investigated they found:

- That raw materials were not being bought by the company direct. The manager had set up a company of his own which bought the raw materials and sold them at a profit to the company; *and*

- That half the factory's sales were not the company's own product but a competitor's cheap and inferior product which the manager was buying in his own name, selling to the company at a profit, repackaging in the company's own bags and selling as theirs.

Of course you and I look at that and think, "Well, the crooked rogue!" But the manager I am talking about did not. His contract did not say he was not allowed to do those things and that meant to him that he was allowed to do them. That is not the attitude of one man only. What is not explicitly excluded is permitted; what is not explicitly included need not be there. So, make sure that your contract/offer/acceptance is as detailed as possible. Say exactly what the packaging will be (if you're placing an order and you want the goods in tubs and the tubs on pallets, say so—otherwise you are likely to get everything loose inside a container).

## Asia-Pacific Economic Cooperation (APEC)

Before we get to individual countries we need to look at APEC. It was formed in 1989 by twelve countries: Australia, Brunei, Canada, Indonesia, Japan, South Korea, Malaysia, New

Zealand, the Philippines, Singapore, Thailand and the USA. If you wonder what some of those countries are doing in a section on South-East Asia, the explanation is that they are all Pacific Rim countries—countries with a coast on the Pacific. Since that start, China, Russia, Mexico, Papua New Guinea, Chile, Peru, Russia and Vietnam have joined. It doesn't take much to see that countries as poor and backward as Papua New Guinea have very little in common with countries as rich and developed as the USA and a lot of APEC's activities have to do with security issues and need not concern us here. Bogor is a city in Indonesia and Busan is another in South Korea, and APEC has a Busan Roadmap to achieve its Bogor Goals. The goals concern free and open trade and investment in the region; the APEC Secretariat puts a brave face on things but they haven't got very far since the goals were established in 1994 and, in my view, they never will—the interests of the various member states are far too disparate. Nevertheless, there are Regional Trading Agreements (RTAs) and Free Trade Agreements (FTAs) that the salesperson needs to be aware of.

## Japan

If there's one country where the advice that you have to go there is true, it's Japan. If they see you regularly your business will increase several times over. The Japanese love quality and they're prepared to pay for it. They have the same committee/consensus approach as I described for the Finns. They also care about face, and this sometimes shows in odd ways. I visited a company in Tokyo with whom we had done business for about ten years, but this time we had some renegotiation to do. I was greeted as cordially as ever but told that the Managing Director would not be able to join us as he was in Osaka, 400 kilometres away. The negotiations were easier than expected and we agreed a new contract both parties were satisfied with, at which point some rapid Japanese (which I do not understand) was spoken and an underling rushed off down the corridor. He was back two minutes later with the

Managing Director, bowing and wreathed in smiles. He had not been teleported from Osaka; he had never been out of the building. The Japanese had not believed we would succeed at the first attempt to negotiate a new deal and the MD was not to be implicated in failure—hence his "absence".

Two travel pointers you might find useful in Japan:

- The Tokyo rail network is wonderfully efficient but difficult for those who don't read Japanese because, although the stations have signs in English, they're swamped by Japanese signs and you can't see them in time. No matter; check before you get on the train what time it is scheduled to arrive at your station. Let's say it's 13.56. When your watch says it's 13.56, get off the train with confidence (as long as your watch keeps correct time) because this *is* your station.

- If you fly into Kansai International Airport at Osaka, be aware that it's on an artificial island built for the purpose. The first time I landed there I didn't know that and it was at night. I could see land and it was over there and not where we were. We got lower and lower and the sea came closer and closer and I was certain we were going down. Why hadn't we been given the "Brace" command? No-one seemed to be panicking so I wasn't going to—I wasn't brought up British and a Queen's Scout for nothing. Ten metres above the sea, I was on my twentieth Hail Mary and suddenly there were lights beneath us; another few seconds and we were over a runway and then we were on it. I put on a languid smile—"I do this all the time"—and looked out of the window at the airport buildings racing by.

## China (including Hong Kong)

While I have operated in China I have not, for some reason, ever worked in Hong Kong but a good friend of mine knows the ex-colony well. What follows is a combination of my input (on China) and his (on Hong Kong).

Don't be afraid to sell to China. You're probably right in your fear that they'll try to reverse engineer or otherwise steal your products but that won't turn them into competitors for a while yet because no-one outside China will believe that a product made there is as good as the same thing produced elsewhere. They're simply going through what the Japanese once did and look at Japan now.

Try to establish a connection with a reliable company on the Chinese mainland. China is as corrupt as anywhere in the world and you need someone to work on your behalf to do whatever fixing needs to be done. Periodic purges of leading Chinese businessmen and officials are dressed up as anti-corruption initiatives. They are not. They usually result from high level power struggles within the regime or the settling of old scores. Western businessmen have sometimes been caught up in these bloodlettings with serious consequences; hence the need to distance yourself from any dirty work that might be going on by working through Chinese intermediaries.

The agreement with China on the future of Hong Kong after the handover of sovereignty by Britain in 1997 guaranteed a high degree of autonomy for the territory except in defence and foreign affairs. This means that Hong Kong exercises executive, legislative and independent judicial powers. It retains its own currency, laws, British common law, and own tax system. It is a free port, separate customs territory and a major international financial centre. It has an excellent and very efficient container port and one of the biggest and most efficient modern airports in the world and was for many years considered one of the best places in the world to do business.

Most Hong Kong manufacturing moved to China years ago and Hong Kong is now mainly a base for companies doing business with China, as well as providing banking and legal services and transhipment facilities for trade with China. There are problems in Hong Kong's the relationship with China, mainly about the degree of influence China seeks to exert over the local Government, but this should not prevent you from doing business in the territory.

## Indonesia

Indonesia is huge and very varied. If you're serious about exporting you have to look at this country—it's the tenth largest economy in the world, has a Gross Domestic Product of $1 trillion and runs a healthy trade surplus thanks to its exports of oil and gas, rubber, textiles and wood products so it has money to spend on your products. There are a lot of rich people but poverty is also widespread—and so are corruption and violence. It's easy to admire Djakarta's wide, sweeping boulevards and they are admirable—but don't lose sight of the fact that they were built for the same reason Napoleon built the ones in Paris: to facilitate troop and armed police movements so that civil disturbance can be controlled quickly. See those tall steel barriers down the middle of the central reservation? The ones set deep into the earth and topped with barbed wire? Gang culture dominates Djakarta and those fences are to keep the gang on this side from getting at the gang on that side because the only result of a collision like that would be multiple deaths. I landed in Djakarta one May Day and found the place thronged with people—men, mostly. 'What's going on?' I asked. I shouldn't have needed to. Djakarta celebrates May Day just as the English peasantry used to, but where the English rustics would have danced round a maypole to promote fertility (and then gone into the bushes to encourage it further), Indonesians go out and find some Chinese to rape and kill. That May Day riot wasn't a particularly noticeable one by local standards—only six Chinese dead at the end of it. A lot of Indonesian Chinese have moved to Australia and who can blame them?

Cash with Order or an irrevocable Letter of Credit are the best ways to deal with Indonesia until you know your customer really well—giving credit is sometimes akin to piling up the money in your yard and setting fire to it.

## Malaysia

The same terms of trade should be used as for Indonesia. Malayisa has Free Trade Agreements with the EU, Australia, New Zealand and a number of other countries and regions but local manufacturers in some industries are still protected by high tariffs, so go to this website to check whether a sales campaign here is likely to be worthwhile:

http://www.miti.gov.my/cms/index.jsp.

Despite the difficulties, Malaysian imports annually from the EU amount to more than €7 billion and US$27 billion from the USA and those are pies it's worth getting a slice of.

## Singapore

After the difficulties of other South East Asian countries, doing business in Singapore is a pleasure. The people are educated, honest and friendly and the government is well disposed towards foreign investment and foreign trade. The language is Malay but English is widely spoken and is, in fact, the main language of business. The legal system is based on English common law. Just don't drop litter in public because it's against the law and the chances of being seen and arrested are very high. Singapore is a free port and most goods (excluding motor vehicles, liquor, tobacco and petroleum products) are imported duty-free. Don't shake hands with a woman unless she offers her hand first (the majority of the Malay population is Moslem). If she does not offer a handshake, bow slightly and place your hand over your heart. You probably need a distributor or agent in Singapore; choose carefully (business in Singapore is in any case rarely rapid) and you will have someone who can advance your business elsewhere in Asia.

# Chapter 8:
# Getting there and staying there

International sales is more expensive than domestic sales because (a) you have to travel further and (b) you will, by and large, find the hotels more expensive than in your own country (obviously, that depends on where your own country is—I'm often appalled by what it costs to stay overnight in the UK compared with, say, France and Germany). One of the things you need to do before you become serious about exporting is set a budget that reflects what it's going to cost you. If you're not prepared to spend the money, you're probably doomed to failure and shouldn't be starting down this road in the first place.

## *Air Travel: Business Class or Economy?*
If you're going to be travelling for more than five hours, ask yourself how pleasant that's going to be in the back of the plane. Then ask yourself whether the budget will allow you to do anything else.

I use Skyscanner http://www.skyscanner.net/ to find the flights I want to use. I just did three searches:

- Return Manchester to Budapest, Economy and Business Class

- Return Manchester to Riyadh, Economy and Business Class

- Return Manchester to Auckland, Economy and

Business Class

In each case I said I'd be flying one week today (if you want to fly this afternoon or even tomorrow you may get some very distorted results) and returning one week later. Here are the results I got:

## Return Manchester to Budapest

Cheapest Economy fare: £104, but this was with an airline I don't use (see below).

Cheapest Economy fare with an airline on my "acceptable" list: £163.

Cheapest Business Class fare: £425.

On the face of it, a Manchester/Budapest flight is short enough that the extra £262 to fly in the front of the plane is not justified—but it isn't that simple. That £163 flight is by Air France through Charles de Gaulle Airport in Paris (CDG) and while the return leg is only five hours and ten minutes, the total journey time on the outward flight is more than twelve hours: you leave Manchester at 19.45, arrive in CDG one and a half hours later and the flight from there to Budapest leaves nine hours after that. So now you have to answer an additional question: am I prepared to spend nine hours in Charles de Gaulle Airport—at night—in order to save £262. So you go further down the list and find that there's a Lufthansa flight for £186 through Munich Airport (MUC) in Germany for which the total journey time in each direction is only four and a half hours including 1hr 20 mins in MUC. So you select that one and you're still saving £239. Except that you're not, because now you have an extra night in the Budapest hotel which you will have to pay for, and a dinner to buy.

## Return Manchester to Riyadh

Cheapest Economy fare: £441. The total journey time on the outward flight is a little over 24 hours and involves stops in CDG and Dubai International Airport (DXB) and, although there is only one stop on the way back (in CDG) the total journey time is still almost 24 hours. In both cases you are going to spend hour after hour in a strange airport. Fancy that? Me neither. So you go down the list looking for the shortest journey time and find that Qatar Airways will get you there in 9hrs 15 mins and bring you back in nine hours at a cost of £935. Most of your time in each direction will be spent in the air but the trip is costing you an extra £494. As far as I'm concerned, you have to be prepared to pay that additional charge because if you don't you're going to arrive in no fit state to work for the first twenty-four hours. And if you're going to go that far, you might as well consider:

Cheapest Business Class Fare: £1,271 by EgyptAir with about three hours in Cairo Airport and total journey time of 10 hrs 30 mins (outward) and 11 hrs 30 mins (return). The Business Class lounge in Cairo is comfortable enough, and now you have to examine whether the extra comfort is worth another £336 on the Qatar Airways flight. That's a personal decision, but I'd say it is—although in my case I'd probably pay an extra £59 and take the Turkish Airlines option through Istanbul at £1,357—nicer lounge and no difference in journey time.

Business Class on EgyptAir and Turkish Airlines is not as comfortable as on, say, long haul Etihad, KLM or Emirates but it's a lot better than Economy and you'll arrive more rested and fitter.

## *Return Manchester to Auckland*

This is a different kettle of fish. If you're flying to New Zealand from the US your journey time is going to range between 13 hours (on Air New Zealand from Los Angeles Airport (LAX)) up to 24 hours (from New York, change at LAX). From pretty well anywhere in Europe it takes longer. You can fly through Singapore, Hong Kong, Dubai, Abu Dhabi, Los Angeles or a few other places but whichever route you choose the journey time will be more than 24 hours. A lot of the people on the flight with you will be on holiday, seeing a place they've dreamed about or visiting family members on a once-in-a-lifetime journey. Economy may be the only option for them. But you're on business and if the potential value of the trip won't pay for a Business Class fare then my advice would be: Don't go.

Fares vary, sometimes wildly, but on the day I checked I found this:

Cheapest Economy fare: £914. That's with China Southern Airlines; it has a total journey time (outbound) of 33 hrs and 55 mins; and there are two stops, one in Amsterdam and one (for nearly eight hours) in Guangzhou International Airport (CAN). I've never flown China Southern and I have no idea what they're like but I know I would not be prepared to make that journey—not even in First Class. It's simply too long. You can do it with Quantas with short changes in DXB and Melbourne Tullamarine Airport (MEL) for £952 but the total journey time is still more than 28 hours going and 29 hours coming back.

Cheapest Business Class Fare: Ignoring all flights with a total journey time in either direction of more than 30 hours, Qantas, Air New Zealand, KLM, Air France or a combination of two or more of those will get you there and back for about £3,700. I'll say it again: If the potential value of the trip won't pay for a Business Class fare, don't go.

## *Which airline?*

Very few airlines are as good as their PR says they are; some are atrocious. There are airlines I like to fly, airlines I fly when I have to, airlines I don't fly and airlines I won't fly and there are airports I avoid whenever I can. Some that were once in the "airlines I like to fly" category are now airlines I don't fly because airlines change over time. This is potentially dangerous ground for me because some airlines might regard what I would say about them as libellous. I could defend it in court but who wants to spend time there? If you Google "airline reviews" you'll find some useful URLs; some of them are:

- Skytrax
  http://www.airlinequality.com/main/forum.htm

- Skyscanner (see above)

- FindTheBest http://airlines.findthebest.com/

One of the items you should take a close look at when you read those reviews is: What is the punctuality like? If a trip involves a change of planes with a short connect time, the airline that is only on time for 70% of its journeys may not be the one you want to book with. There's an airline that has been one of my favourites for at least the past five years; I have their gold frequent flyer card and six months ago I could not conceive of wanting to change—but I have flown with them eight times in the past five months and every single one of those flights has taken off and landed anywhere from forty minutes to more than two hours late. They're not cheap, they have built a reputation as one of the world's best airlines since they were formed early this century and until recently I thought they were the best in the world—but now I'm taking a break from them. I'll come back in six months and see if they've improved. If not, they'll have moved onto my list of airlines I don't fly.

It's also a good idea, if your trip involves more than one flight, to think about where the airline's hub is. Austrian Airlines fly through Vienna; Lufthansa mostly through Frankfort but also through Munich or Dusseldorf; British Airways through London Heathrow or London Gatwick; Etihad through Abu Dhabi; Emirates through Dubai; United through no fewer than nine US airports—and so on. One of the reasons I like flying Lufthansa is that German airports are like the rest of Germany—everything works as it's supposed to. And, by the same token, I stay away from Austrian Airlines (unless Vienna is my destination) to avoid the nightmare that Vienna International Airport can be for transit passengers. Istanbul Airport is even worse than Vienna for those in transit;

# John Lynch

Turkish Airlines sometimes offers peachy deals and they need to to overcome the negative effect of knowing that you have to go through Istanbul.

When you're booking flights, check all of the details. Can the ticket be changed or cancelled? If so, at what fee? If I think there's the slightest chance that I will have to change my flight arrangements after I've booked, I make sure I have a ticket that allows changes either free or for a modest charge. That will often cost more, but sometimes the cheapest ticket can't be changed or cancelled at all—if you find you can't use the fight on the day and at the time you booked for, you lose the money.

And *how* do you get a refund? In one case I encountered recently, you can book and change bookings online but to cancel a flight you have to go to the airline's office—which, for me, would involve a round trip of nearly 200 miles. When you get there, you have to give them your bank account details: the sort code, account number, account name—and the IBAN code! I could get the code, number and name off my debit card, but who on earth carries their IBAN code around with them? I suggested to the person behind the counter that this was a way to get customers to give up; I did not get an answer.

How much cabin baggage and how much checked luggage are you allowed? If you want to take more, can you? And at what cost?

Something else to remember about cancellations is that, if you cancel one part of a booking, all subsequent parts are almost always automatically cancelled. Example: You book a return flight to Nairobi but then you discover that you need to be in Dubai around that time. No problem, you think; you'll book a single to Dubai, another single from there to Nairobi and you'll have the return half of the ticket you originally booked to Nairobi to come back on. Well, no, you won't—because the minute you fail to get on the outward flight to Nairobi (whether you've cancelled it or not), the whole of the rest of that ticket is cancelled. You may get some kind of refund but you'll have to book a new flight home and that's when you'll find that booking a one way flight is very often not a lot cheaper than buying a return.

Any decent airline today should give you the chance to choose your seat at the time of booking and you should use it. Business Class or Economy, I always prefer to fly in an aisle seat; you may have a different preference but whatever it is you like, choose it now—and, if you possibly can, check in on-line at the earliest possible time (generally—but not invariably—24 hours before scheduled take-off time) to make sure you've got the seats you wanted.

## *Hotels*

Hotels can chew up huge chunks of your budget if you let them. You need to define what you look for in an hotel. If it's the appearance of five star luxury and a name you can drop in conversation with people you hope to impress, you should probably skip the rest of this section because that isn't what I look for.

Ask the people you're going to visit what hotel they recommend. Also ask if they have a corporate rate and, if they do, get them to make the booking for you. Other people to ask are friends and colleagues who may have travelled there before—but be sure they understand what you're looking for as it may not be the same as what they wanted in an hotel.

Then take a look at Tripadvisor. I know that there are lots of tendentious or indeed false reviews on Tripadvisor but I use the site and I think it's easy enough to tell the ones that are meant from the ones that are there to score points, damage a competitor, boost a friend's hotel or get revenge on a restaurant that insisted you pay the full bill when you complained (after eating every bite).

What would be important to you on holiday and what matters on a business trip are different things. I suggest you should be looking for:

- A location close to the people you plan to visit;

- A reliable WiFi connection;

- Security (depending on how dangerous the country you're in appears to be);

- A Business Centre with, at the very least, the ability to photocopy documents and to print from a flash drive;

- Laundry and dry cleaning facilities if you're going to be there more than two or three days;

- A restaurant good enough to entertain customers in if necessary;

- A lobby in which you can buy a customer coffee without having to go to your room; *and*

- A room comfortable enough to relax in and quiet enough to sleep.

How you rank those points in your own mind is a matter personal to you, but you need them all. I value restaurant quality above room luxury—here is a Tripadvisor review I wrote in 2012 on Al Bilad Hotel in Jeddah:

Albilad Hotel isn't Five Star and it doesn't pretend to be. It's an honest Four Star hotel that does its best for its customers. Breakfast is fine and evening meals are good -- I and a guest ate the barbecue one night [barbecue in the Middle East doesn't mean what it means in most of the West) and we were really pleased by quality, service and price. Wireless email wasn't working in my room but I'm assured it usually is. There was no safe in my room and I do think a safe is necessary. Nevertheless, it's a good business hotel and I'll be staying there again. Overall, I think it sets out to appeal even more to local people wanting coffee or a meal and that means the food offer may be a little better than the room offer, but the rooms are fine.

When I read through this review I seem to be damning with faint praise -- but what you need to remember is that there aren't any good hotels in Jeddah -- I mean that; there are none -- and this one competes well while being half the price of some I could mention. Stay here. You won't be disappointed.

I've stayed at Al Bilad several times since then and it has gone up in my estimation. The rooms are old and somewhat shabby and there's still no safe, but WiFi always works now. What makes the place stand out is the food and especially the seafood: hammour and nagil fresh out of the Red Sea the day you eat them. I've stayed in other, more expensive, Jeddah hotels and I always come back to this one. But here's what someone else wrote in the same place about the same hotel:

Rooms are very old, some of them they never get fully dry as humidity took over long time ago. Noise is continuous, they are renovating for more than a year, drilling and hammering starts at 10 am everyday, sometimes hot water is missing for one or more days. They have an arab wedding room and they use it quite often, this will bring music loud up to 4 am. Food is average and quite expensive. Reception staff is sometimes friendly sometimes not, I have been answered that was not their problem if I have to work early morning and the "disco" was fully on just one wall away from my room. Internet is quite slow. Definitely better to find another place.

So, you pays your money and you takes your choice. There are hotels in Jeddah like the Crowne Plaza which will give you more luxury and better rooms but when I checked today I found room-only prices for my next visit ranging between 875 and 1,173 Saudi Riyals per night; I pay 530 Riyals Bed and Breakfast at Al Bilad—and in my experience the food in the Crowne Plaza is not better than it is in Al Bilad.

My favourite hotels in other places (some a lot more luxurious and a lot pricier than Al Bilad) include: the Fairview in Nairobi; the Four Seasons in Damascus; the Hyatt Regency in Djakarta; and the Beach Rotana in Abu Dhabi. Google them and you'll see a wide range of hotel types, so what I guess it says is that you need to get to know what you really like in an hotel and then take the time to find places that meet your needs. (My favourite hotel anywhere, ever, used to be the Taj Mahal in Mumbai that was burned down by terrorists. The older "heritage" section was particularly wonderful).

It's worth remembering that your idea of what's funny may not chime with someone else's. I checked into a swanky hotel in South East Asia and had been in my room for twenty minutes when the phone rang. Would I, the concierge wanted to know, like a nice young lady to join me there? I thanked him for his kindness but said that, on the assumption that she would be neither nice nor a lady and quite possibly only too young, I'd pass. 'Oh,' he said. 'You want I find you old woman?'

## Insurance

You need it. It's very easy to assume that your normal company insurance covers you, but check. Insurance companies hate paying out and they will do all they can to resist a claim; you don't want to find after you have submitted one that they would happily have paid you if only you'd told them where you were going before you went there but, as it is…

Medical insurance should cover you for treatment as out-patient or in hospital and for all the other costs—accommodation, food, drugs—that can go with that. You also, though, need cover that will pay to bring you home (in a specially equipped aircraft or with a qualified person accompanying you) should that be necessary. I've been hospitalised only twice in over forty years. The first time, my company paid the hospital direct and then flew me home. The second time, the hospital carried out all sorts of irrelevant tests while I was unconscious and were preparing to inflict more on me when I woke up. This was simply a way of jacking up my bill—none of the tests was necessary but all of them cost money—and I checked myself out, booked a flight home and didn't tell the airline that something unpleasant would be dripping onto the seat from the back of my head all through the seven hour flight (sorry, Airline). In that case my customer paid the hospital bill, my employer reimbursed the customer and our insurance company refunded the money to us.

If the worst happens, your insurance should pay to bring your body home for burial.

Whether you want insurance against flight cancellations and delays is up to you and your company; I've always simply submitted the extra expense claim that resulted and my employer has paid it but it might be wise to ask your own company to confirm that they're happy with that approach.

If you go to Libya, Iraq and one or two other countries, you need Kidnap and Ransom Insurance. I talk about taking care of yourself in places like that in Chapter 7.

# Chapter 9:
# What Can Go Wrong?

## Scams

Scams are as prevalent in export sales as they are in lots of other things.

### Example 1

Someone telephones you from Uganda and asks the ex works price of one of your products. You tell him. He says he'll take one and a friend of his who happens to be in your country (and flying home this evening) will stop by to pick it up. You say, "Hold on, we don't know you, it will have to be cash up front," and he says, "No problem, email me your bank details and I'll get the money transferred today". An hour later, he emails you a copy of a bank transfer showing that the money is on its way to your account. The email is from a yahoo address but you know that's often true of genuine customers in Africa. You compare the transfer document with others you've received that proved to be good and it looks genuine. Your bank details are correct and it tells you the name of the customer's bank (you Google it to make sure it really exists) and it names the account being debited and the amount being transferred. You also Google the name of the customer on the transfer advice and you can see that you're dealing with a company of reasonable size, in business for twenty years and respected in its field.

The friend turns up and asks for the package. You're not entirely comfortable with letting it go until the money reaches your account, but experience says that's going to take a couple of days and this man has a plane to catch. You hand over the goods.

When the money hasn't arrived after three days, you telephone the company named on the payment advice. They ask you to quote their order number. You say you don't have one. They say they never heard of the person whose name you mention, they didn't want the goods you sell and nor do they have them and as for paying for them—forget it. Then they hang up.

Whether your original caller impersonated a genuine company or whether it really was the genuine company that contacted you doesn't matter. Unless you send someone to Uganda to spy on the company, and unless that person is able to photograph your goods in the company's possession, you're not going to get paid. You broke some of the fundamental rules of selling:

- Know your Customer;

- Even if you do know your customer, make sure you have a contract and that the customer knows and accepts your terms and conditions; *and*

- Cash with Order should mean what it says.

You had the first signal that all might not be as it seemed when a man you didn't know telephoned from a company you'd never heard of and told you that he needed something in a great hurry. Hurry is always a sign of possible danger. If you sell to contractors then you're accustomed to rush orders because they won't order what they need until they've been awarded the contract and then they want to start work immediately, but in this case they could have contacted you when the man set off for your country and they didn't do that—they waited till he was about to leave for home (or that's what they told you). What you needed to do was to fax them a quotation and a copy of your terms and conditions of business and ask them to fax or email back to you a signed copy. You should also, when you Googled the company, have gone to the Contact Us page to see whether it shows email addresses that identify the company (e.g. info@companyname.ug) and, if it did, you should have asked for the confirming email to come from that address. Finally, you should have sent the payment advice to your bank and asked them to get the Ugandan bank's confirmation that it was genuine. Anyone with a fully-featured version of Adobe Acrobat can mock up (or modify) a pdf document and save it as a JPEG, and that's probably how the transfer advice you received was created.

In the last resort, if you couldn't complete all of those steps, you should not have allowed yourself to be rushed into releasing the goods. Yes, you could lose the business—wouldn't that have been better than losing the money? (Something every salesperson should be asked, when he wants to push through an order, is: If we lose this amount of money, what volume of sales do we then have to do at the margins we are currently achieving to generate enough profit to cover the cost of the loss? In other words, just to stand still?) And you probably wouldn't have lost the business anyway, if it had been genuine.

## Example 2

A while ago I received an email that purported to come from the General the American Forces in Iraq. Attached to it was a letter on convincing letterhead advising us that the Unified Command had a great deal of money to spend on products like ours and asking for quotations for large volumes of material.

The letter was convincing, the need for the material was likely and we had shipped it to Iraq in the past. When I Googled the sender's name I found that he was who he said he was. I prepared the quotation. However, when I came to send it I noticed that the email address the supposed General was using was nowhere near Iraq, and nor was it in the USA. I held onto the quotation and forwarded the original email to our Embassy in Baghdad, asking if they would mind checking it out. They didn't mind at all and were able to tell me within the day that the General knew nothing about the inquiry sent in his name, that they were not at that time looking for material like ours and, if they were, that the request for prices would come from somewhere else entirely. I replied to the original email, drawing attention to the disconnect between his supposed office and the email address he was using and declining to quote. I heard no more.

However, a few weeks later someone elsewhere in our company received a very similar inquiry. He sent it to me, Iraq being on my patch. I replied to the inquiry saying, in effect: Look, we know this is a scam, we've seen it before and we'd rather not see it again so please take us off whatever database you're using. Once again, we heard no more.

The lesson: Don't be put off by emails that come to you with a yahoo, GMail or Hotmail address because in some parts of the world genuine companies are using those. However, you must examine very carefully the communications you receive and, if there is any hint of something that is not as you would expect it to be, you must check. Scams are getting cleverer. I'm not the first person to say that, if some scammers I have encountered put as much effort into honest business enterprise as they do into trying to defraud people, they would be legitimately rich.

## Example 3

There's a version of Example 2 that goes to the other extreme—instead of a high-flown job title and a letter encrusted with seals, you get an email like this (I actually received this on the very day that I am writing this chapter. The names have been changed to protect the guilty):

*Good Day,*

*I am Ima Bigcheese by name, the C.E.O of a newly Established Store and General Merchandise here in xxxxx. I will (sic) like to place an order with you/your company but need to know some of your company policy as have some questions to ask you, below are the question:*

# The International Sales Handbook

*1. Do you allow Email Order*

*2. Do you Accept Credit Card (Visa, Master, Amex or Discover) as the Means of Payment.*

*3. Do you Ship Internationally or Can I arrange the pick up with my a shipping company after the payment is been confirmed*

*Kindly get back to me immediately with your website or the price list of your present stock list products so I email your the list along with the quantities needed.*

*Hope to read from you now.*

*Regards*

*Dr Ima Bigcheese*

*Director/C.E.O*

*B.I.G.store Inc.*

I don't know where Dr Bigcheese was really emailing from and I wasn't sufficiently interested to ask our IT people to trace it back. I replied very politely, telling him where he could find our website but not quoting any prices; I finished with this: *To this I will add only that we would need some concrete information about your company before being prepared to quote prices. For example, when you say "here in xxxxx"—where exactly in xxxxx? You will understand that a company operating around the world, as we do, is the object of frequent scams and—while I would not for a moment suspect you of being involved in such a thing—we do have checking processes that we must follow.* The point of that, of course, was to make clear that I knew exactly what he was up to and it wasn't going to work.

## Example 4

A scam that seems particularly popular in parts of Africa involves placing an order, sending too much money to your account by bank transfer and immediately sending a politely flustered email explaining how their accounts department mixed up two invoices and sent you the wrong amount. If you'll just be good enough to refund the difference to their account, everything will be fine. Well, *don't* refund the difference because everything *won't* be fine. Don't ship the goods, either. Within 48 hours, you will find that the original payment has gone from your account, recalled by the scammer's bank, and your money will be gone, too. If you find yourself in this position—order received, too much money in your account, request for refund of difference—send a polite reply saying, "We prefer not to confuse payments in this way. We will ask our bank to return your money to you, less any charges they may impose. We suggest that you then send us the correct amount; when we have received it, we will release the order." You won't, in fact, receive the correct amount but if you do then wait at least four days after receipt before releasing the goods, to make sure the money stays in your account.

## *Failure to communicate*

You are dealing with people whose first language is not your own and sometimes it will be difficult to understand what is being said. Make sure you remove the doubt. What, for example, do you suppose this means?

> *Dear John*
>
> *was transferred 20% of the total amount of the bill, but there was a problem today that required a white pigment and yellow note I am not you convert 20%*
>
> *Regards*

The background is that we had agreed a sale, total value $160,000 payable 20% Cash with Order and the balance by Cash against Documents. The statement "was transferred 20% of the total amount of the bill" is clear enough—they have asked their bank to send us $32,000, or 20% of the total—but what was I to make of "there was a problem today that required a white pigment and yellow note I am not you convert 20%"? In fact, I could guess what he meant—but guessing is exactly what you should not do in a situation like this because, if you guess wrong, you have a potential can of worms. What I did, therefore, was to email him and say, "Are you saying that the whole shipment should now be white and that the yellow you required is not now needed? If so, does the amount of the white product remain as it was or do I increase it by replacing the amount of yellow product with a similar amount of white?" He replied that the second option was what he wanted but that was still not enough—I sent him a revised pro forma invoice setting out the sale as I now understood he wanted it and asked him to sign it and send it back to me. This was particularly important in this case as his country requires pre-inspection of imported goods (see Chapter 2) and, if we had not obtained confirmation of the revised order, the inspection company would have refused to sign off the shipment because it did not conform to the order. However, even where inspection is not required you should protect yourself in all cases where payment is not Cash with Order by making sure that the order you have on file, signed by the customer, is the order you are shipping.

That was a specific case; the general rule should always be not to guess what the customer wants but to get it confirmed. (That also applies when the customer amends any aspect of the order with a phone call—confirm it. Always).

## *Incorrect Packaging and/or Documentation*

I talked about packaging in Chapter 2. Here's an example of what can go wrong. Shipping goods to another country is not the same as shipping the same goods domestically. Your shipment is going to be inspected by Customs officials and they need to see what they expect to see. I mentioned in Chapter 5 the problems that arose when beads were put in empty paint tins "for safety". Remember: what it says on the documents has to be what appears in the container or on the pallets. In situations like this I usually find myself sighing and saying, "Ask how much he wants"—an approach that is now illegal under anti-corruption legislation (see Chapter 3, Corruption).

## *Failure to get paid*

### Customer can't pay

This can be a problem with domestic sales, too, but international sales present special difficulties because you can't usually turn up and recover the goods. I know this will seem unhelpful but the best advice I can offer is: don't get into this position in the first place. The approval of credit for overseas customers should be a shade tighter than for domestic sales. If you would find a customer slightly iffy if he lived in the street next to yours but you're just about prepared to offer him thirty days credit, tell a similar customer in another country that you need cash in advance. Yes, you may lose sales but, as I've said elsewhere, what every salesperson should take into account is: if we end up writing this amount off, how much do I have to sell at our current margins just to cover that loss? With margins where they are right now, that can be a sobering calculation.

### Incorrect documentation

A customer who isn't good for the money is not the only reason for non-payment. Your documentation has to be correct in all respects. With export sales, it isn't only the customer who needs to be happy—the customer's bank, the central bank in the customer's country, the Customs officers clearing imports and the inspection company (if there is one) all need to be satisfied that the documents are correct. And to that list, if payment is by Letter of Credit, you can add the advising bank, which may be your bank and may not.

### Incorrect Goods

This is self-explanatory, but important. You wouldn't expect to pay for the wrong goods, so why should your customer? The reason it's important is because it brings me back to something I've said before:

if you want to succeed as an exporter, the whole company has to understand what that means and everyone has to buy into it. I quoted on the previous page an example of the goods being right but the documentation wrong. Getting the documentation right and the goods wrong is as bad and I had a nasty example with a sale to South Africa. The order was in tonnes (twenty of them), South Africa being a metric country, but the product was to be shipped from America where a ton is only 2,000 pounds compared to the 2,240 pounds in a metric tonne. The logistics department in the States assured me there'd be no problem—the factory in Texas would be told to ship twenty pallets each containing 2,240 pounds. I know they were told that, because I saw the order document sent to them. The factory manager, though, knew better. He'd been making this product for ten years; he'd shipped it all over the USA; every shipment had been in tons of 2,000 pounds each and no-one had ever complained. These South Africans didn't know what they were talking about; and where was South Africa anyways? Somewhere down Alabama way, probably, and every Texan knows what that means.

We ended up shipping 4,800 pounds after the first shipment, on two pallets. The customer was not amused. We rescued him from the clutches of the competition, because that's what salespeople do, but we paid a price and the price was: no more shipments from America. You use a European plant or we go elsewhere.

The only way to avoid this sort of self-inflicted injury is to train all of your staff in what it means to be an exporter, what their role in the process is and how they can best execute it.

## *Clash of Cultures*

I said elsewhere that other people's religion and other people's politics are not your business. We all grow up taking for granted that the way things are done where we are is the "normal" or "proper" way. It can come as a surprise to learn that people brought up far away in other cultures think that their habits and beliefs, which are very different from ours, are the correct ones. If you want an example just look at what happens when the West attempts to give other lands the glorious benefit of democracy.

This doesn't have to be a problem—I've thought for a long time that if everyone had to spend two years or so living and working in a culture completely different from their own then peace might finally descend on the world—but it often is. A thoughtless sentence; an opinion you never intended to convey; the suggestion that all would be well if the target country would just adopt British/American/German ways and all thoughts of doing business with you are drowned out in the prospect's mind by outrage at your arrogance.

The solution: leave your opinions where they grew—at home. You don't need to pretend to adopt those of your hosts. They'll know you don't mean it. Just accept that some topics are off limits.

## Sudden Shocks

In May 2014 I accepted an order from a customer in Baghdad. We'd done business with this customer in the past and we were happy to agree the terms that had always worked before of 20% Cash with Order and the balance Cash Against Documents. (Don't waste time trying to get a Letter of Credit out of an Iraqi bank. They'll issue one but it will be riddled with errors and you won't be able to use it). The order wasn't huge—about $150,000 CiF Umm Qasr—but any sum of money is too much to lose. During June, the situation in Iraq deteriorated badly. The bank's advice was: Change the terms to Cash In Advance. Yes, well, thank you, Bank, but if you really did know the things your advertising says you do then you'd know that the Iraqi Central Bank makes it almost impossible for importers to transmit the bulk or all of the value of a transaction before they have evidence that the goods have actually been shipped. Iraqis don't trust anyone—their own people or the rest of the world.

This is where your forwarder comes into his own (or, in our case, her own) and it illustrates why I said as long ago as Chapter 1 that your choice of forwarder should be based on performance and experience and not on price. The shipment wasn't going direct to Umm Qasr; it was being transhipped in Jebel Ali, so there was time to have the goods shipped to an alternative consignee if it looked as though delivery was becoming too risky. Don't be afraid to abort if that's what the situation dictates. (In the case I've just described we were paid without difficulty).

## *Kidnap*

Kidnap is not particularly common, but it happens. I'm afraid the best advice I can give is: Don't let it happen to you.

Two men tried to kidnap me at Murtala Muhammed International Airport in Lagos, Nigeria by pretending that they'd been sent by my hotel to collect me. It wasn't the most professional attempt—there are never two drivers in the same taxi and the fact that another driver was also holding up a card with my name on it raised questions in my mind. I got the driver on his own to show me his ID and car and then I rang my hotel: 'There's a man here called x driving a car with the licence plate y; is he yours?' They confirmed that he was and I let the other two see me wave at a policeman to catch his attention. They faded away with no further bother. But people have been kidnapped from outside that airport and they've later turned up dead, so be vigilant. Make sure a car is waiting for you and make sure that the one you're invited to get into really is that car.

There was also an attempt in Qatar, of all places—you don't expect it there and I still don't know whether it was an ordinary criminal attempt or a contractor I had crossed swords with looking to have me done away with. In either case, I simply followed the rule I mentioned in Chapter 7—don't get into a car unless:

- You were expecting it;

- You know the driver or have other proof that this is the car you were expecting;

## John Lynch

- You know where you're going; *and*

- Someone else knows where you are and who you're with.

If you have kidnap and ransom insurance, carry the emergency contact number with you at all times. If things go wrong, you are kidnapped and your kidnappers look like people with little respect for human life, tell them as soon as possible that you are insured and that they will only collect if they hand you over alive, and give them the contact number. Good luck.

## Author's Note

I hope you have found this handbook useful. If you want to contact me, you can do so by email at rjl@mandrillpress.com or you can find me on my blog at www.jlynchblog.com or on the publisher's website www.mandrillpress.com.

# Appendix 1

## *The Trap of Apparently High Market Price*

Your research tells you that the going market price for a product similar to yours delivered to the customer is $1,000 (each; per tonne or ton (they're not the same); per 1,000 litre tank—whatever). Your ex works price of $500 gives you a 25% margin. You can get 20 (units; tons; tanks—whatever) in a 20 foot container and the cost of freight from your factory to the entry port for the target market is $3,500 so—provided that you can ship in full container loads—the freight adds $175 to each unit, ton or OPC. Insurance is another $2.20, which is scarcely worth worrying about—but you'd better not forget that you need it. So the price cif the port of entry (cif means cost, insurance and freight) amounts to a total of $677, which means you can easily undercut that $1,000 market price. You could even stick on another $100 and sell at $777, giving you a price tag like a Boeing and a better margin than the 25% you're making at home. Why didn't you do this before?

Except, of course, that you can't sell at that price because there are some things you haven't yet taken into account. $677 gets your goods to the dockside; the $1,000 market price is delivered to customer. So, you need to add import duty; clearance costs and carriage to the final destination. Import duty is 15%, so your $677 goes to $780. You're bringing in a container of twenty, but customers buy one at a time so the first thing you need to do is move the whole container to your warehouse and unload it.

Of course, you don't yet have a warehouse because this is a new venture. So you rent one. You'll find out later—too late, because when you rented the warehouse the landlord insisted on you taking a two-year lease—that the warehouse is in completely the wrong place. Your biggest customers are so far away from it that internal freight (the cost of moving the goods from the docks, or from your warehouse, to their final destination) eats into your profit margin which is, in any case, nothing like the figure you thought it would be.

The rent is not the only cost when you take on a warehouse. You need security—either a watchman or a service provided by a security company. You need someone to count the goods in and out and make sure that the quantity you have is the quantity you're supposed to have. You probably need racking. You may well need a fork-lift, which means you also need a fork-lift driver. Now you need some way to split those additional costs across the product so that you can estimate what your true costs are going to be, so you have to assume a minimum sales volume. The usual—and possibly best— method is to evaluate the total market size and assume that your initial share of that market will be a low one. So, let us assume: that you sell your product in units (rather than tons, tonnes, gallons or anything else); that your research says the country you are looking at absorbs 1 million units p.a.; and that, although you will be aiming for a 15% market share (150,000 units) in Year 1, for the sake of this exercise you are going to take a worst case scenario and calculate on the assumption that you won't get more than 5% market share (50,000 units). Now you know how to split up the additional costs you will incur during the first year: you divide them by 50,000 and that's the amount you have to add to the cif value for each unit—the $780 we talked about earlier.

Finally, you will approach three haulage companies and ask what they would charge to transport your goods from your warehouse to the places you expect your customers to be. You won't necessarily choose the lowest quote—what you need is the company that will most cost-effectively provide the level of service you need and your customers demand.

Job done. You have established exactly what it will cost to get your product from your own factory and across the sea to this new market, calculated on the most conservative of assumptions. You know how much you can sell it for when you get it there. Deduct cost from selling price and you have your profit on each unit. What could possibly go wrong?

Quite a lot, actually. Here is a list (by no means exhaustive) of things that can make you wish you'd never heard of this country, let alone tried to sell to it:

- That selling price you found when you were researching the general market price level. You assumed it represented the same sort of margin to other sellers as it would to you. You were wrong.

- As we have demonstrated, $1,000 per unit represents a fairly small margin to you, but you're manufacturing in America.

- Your biggest competitor in the new market manufactures in China. Or Malaysia. Or India. Your labour costs are not as high as they would be in Europe, but they're a lot higher than the other guy's.

- You both use the same raw materials, so at least those costs will be the same—yes? Well, perhaps not. Many raw materials suppliers operate zonal pricing, where exactly the same product is sold in different parts of the world at very different prices.

- You are subject to regulation and restriction (Health & Safety; pollution control; working hours; and so many more) that push your costs up but which your competitors in many countries don't have to trouble themselves with.

The fact is that the delivered-to-customer selling price that gives you a 25% margin represents a 55% margin to your competition. You come on the scene and they cut their prices to a level 10% below yours. They still have an acceptable margin; you are in deep trouble. The Moral: what you called research, I call guesswork. You have to get your facts right before you jump in and not through being taught painful lessons.

- When you rented that warehouse, did you research all the legalities that might be involved? Most countries (not all) allow a foreign entity to sell direct in their country provided that all they do is ship the goods and hand the Bills of Lading and other documents to a person or company in their country so that that person or company can clear them. Once you enter into a commercial transaction—and renting a warehouse is exactly that—there may be legal formalities you have to observe. You may not (though you may) have to go all the way and set up a company in the country but you probably still have to register in some way. If you do, there are costs; if you don't, you may have imported stock that you now can't sell. ***The Moral:*** I have a lot more to say about research in the chapter called, oddly enough, *Research*. Please. Read it. More than once.

- The market into which you are selling is corrupt. Your product doesn't sell there because you're not paying off the right people. ***The Moral:*** see Chapter 3.

What do you do if you're trying to enter a market by undercutting the established suppliers and it isn't working? Go back to Chapter 2, Things to be aware of before you sign up, go to the heading You do it their way—not yours and then to the sub-heading Do you have something new to offer? Or simply a Me-Too? and read my suggestions there.

# Appendix 2

## *What may be found in a Submittal*

Title: *What the submittal is for, who is submitting it and to whom. Name or other identification details of the project.*

Covering Letter: *Describe what you are submitting.*

Scope of Work: *Make absolutely clear what is included in the work you propose to do or the product(s) you propose to supply—you don't want any differences of opinion later as to what should actually have been provided for the price.*

Price and Terms of Payment

Technical Specification: *Include the national/international standards relevant to the project and show compliance. Make sure that all of the products that will be involved are listed and the technical data supplied. Provide laboratory certificates where applicable together with manufacturer's ISO certificates.*

Method Statement: *If you are bidding for work rather than to supply product(s) give a detailed account of how the work would be carried out.*

Reference Sites: *Provide a list of where you have carried out similar work in the past/customers to whom you have supplied the product(s).*

# Appendix 3

## *Typical Response to a Submittal*

| Name of Employer | Name of Project<br>*Construction of Research Complex - Phase 1* | Name of Construction Manager |
|---|---|---|

### The CM's Reply to Submittals

| Submittal Number | Date |
|---|---|
| Submittal Title | |
| Contractor's Name | Contract Number |
| Action Code (tick as appropriate) | |

- ☐ 1. Approved. Work may proceed
- ☐ 2. Approved as noted, work may proceed subject to incorporation of comments and resubmittal
- ☑ 3. Revise and resubmit, work may not proceed
- ☐ 4. Rejected
- ☐ 5. Review not required

**Review comments**
1. The material specification from the manufacturer do not match those in the project specifications
2. The colours referred to in the submittal do not include all required colours
3. Manufacturer describes two application methods that may be used. Manufacturer is required to specify which method shall be used

Please provide more information on packaging and storage

# Index

Lightning Source UK Ltd.
Milton Keynes UK
UKOW05f1234101014

239914UK00006B/74/P